*To the founders and leaders building
companies designed for humans*

SCALE
WITHOUT LOSING YOUR SOUL

SIMON D'ARCY
& TODD EMAUS

SCALE WITHOUT LOSING YOUR SOUL
The Startup Culture Guide

ISBN PAPERBACK: 978-1-5445-3728-3
      EBOOK: 978-1-5445-3729-0

CONTENTS

FOREWORD

Iconic, high-growth companies have two things in common: they are (a) in a chaotic (and energizing) mode of rapid scale, and (b) they fear losing what is unique and special, their essence.

We all know these iconic companies when they make it: they are known for not only their product or service but their culture as well. Often they've become fertile grounds for employee talent. These companies have a defined sense of who they are at an almost intangible level, an essence that is one part culture and one part brand. This essence comes from their founders, the distinctions of their product, and the early overlay of their organizational DNA. They have taken the time to know themselves at a deep level, which becomes their brand externally and their culture internally. They tend to build organizational processes in-house and rarely pull best practices off of the shelf. These companies know subtleties matter, and just because one company did a certain process like performance management or feedback a certain way doesn't mean the exact application will work at their company. Even though there are commonalities in high-performing companies and cultures, the differences matter and provide a guide to create a coherent operating system through the stages of organizational growth. Each tribe of humans has their own defined essence, and businesses are just another version of the tribe or community that supports the life of the business.

At Evolution—a coaching and leadership consulting firm that supports high-growth startups to scale up from the inside out—we have been blessed to participate in the discovery and the integration of essence within many of these companies. They include tech companies like Slack, Twitter, Dropbox, Iterable, and Glassdoor, as well as healthcare companies such as Cricket Health, Radiology Partners, and National Veterinary Associates. They have all taken a more direct approach to understanding themselves and their essence, building culture as they grew.

We don't take this responsibility lightly. We know that their destiny is their own and that we are merely guides in helping them grow into who they must become. The metaphor is the same for a child growing up: each one has an acorn inside that, with the right conditions, can grow into their own version of a mighty oak.

Many companies, however, don't make it, and more than we know never break past certain organizational stages: staying in the garage with an idea, not growing beyond a small founding team with a product, or the early stages of growth with fewer than fifty people. The road of startups is littered with examples of companies that haven't made it. Many couldn't get past co-founder misalignment, many had the wrong product/market fit, and many lacked the clarity around who they were.

One of the admirable traits of Stewart Butterfield, the founder and CEO of Slack, was his ability to learn from his past experience at Flickr to Yahoo, which influenced him to take a very intentional approach to his second founding with Slack. He was motivated to do culture right and focus on the essence of what made Slack distinctive, including all sorts of rich narratives and stories he told to illustrate what made Slack special. One was a somewhat reductive and cheeky maxim, "This is a place of business," which meant the usual startup trappings of foosball tables and such weren't as prominent, and everything was geared toward helping people do their jobs. Then there was the related "Work hard and go home." Slack made an explicit point to not provide dinner at the office. This was meant to encourage employees to finish their work and not stay into the evening. He referenced seeing a hunting dog joyously supporting hunters on an outdoors trip and would say "Be the dog" as a way to align a person with what they were meant to do in the world, following their intrinsic sense of purpose. These are examples of subtle and important principles connected to real actions—all of which built culture.

Our clients often become our long-term partners as we learn with them, helping them discover their DNA and embed it in everything to create a system that replicates the best of itself. Recruiting filters, feedback systems, management training, organizational communications, and office design are a few of the levers that can be pulled to create a coherent sense of culture. It isn't just done in the good times, either, as culture is far more than fun and foosball tables. It is everything down to the soul of the company itself. It is led symbolically every day by leaders of all types and needs constant reinforcement as a social mechanism to guide humans at work. Culture is organizational anthropology in the best sense, and the study of how groups of people are different and function in the world works the same in business.

Simon D'Arcy and Todd Emaus are Evolution partners on the journey and with wisdom to share. They have both had extensive experience both in the seat in scaling organizations and supporting culture development in rapidly scaling companies. They are two of the best culture-builders out there, and I am privileged to learn with them every day. I think you will find them as engaging, creative, and passionate as our clients do, and I hope that you undergo your own journey as you move through these pages and undertake the journey yourself to discover how businesses can be more than just drivers of revenue, but engines of value that are unordinary in their quest to be truly special places. Enjoy reading, and we hope to learn with you as we collectively find new ways of creating world-enriching value through business together.

MATT AURON
Managing Director and Co-Founder, Evolution
November 2022

INTRODUCTION

It's hard to build a successful company. More than 90 percent of all startups fail. Those that raise venture capital only mildly increase their likelihood of survival, as 75 percent of venture-backed startups don't ever return cash to their investors.

The odds are stacked against you from the beginning.

And most of those that make it never realize their full potential. The business scales, but at the expense of deeply held values. The things that matter most—the principles by which we choose to live and work—become secondary. Growth becomes primary. At best, the company becomes yet another ordinary startup. At worst, it grows into another soul-crushing place of work.

The worst offenders are exposed in the media, with stories recounting regular harassment, sexism, racism, brutal expectations around work hours, and alcohol-fueled workplaces. Some of us have had the experience of working for companies like these. Maybe we have even sworn to never do that again.

But the fate of most companies is neither fame nor infamy. It is mediocrity. Just another in a long line of places to go to work.

These types of companies have become so commonplace that many of us take for granted that this is how businesses typically grow. The early days are exciting, fun, and filled with purpose. Then, as the company scales, the good times fade away. Bureaucracy, power struggles, and an overemphasis of the bottom line take over.

Fortunately, there is another way. Few companies find it. Fewer dare to explore it.

This other way begins with a decision to create more than just another business: to build a company and a culture where people can do the best work of their lives. A place where you yourself would want to work. A workplace filled with meaning and potential. A workplace that stands for something more than just profit.

This book is for leaders who make that decision, leaders who want to scale without losing their soul.

Whether your organization is small or already well into scaling, you're holding a proven guide for building a vibrant culture at your company.

Imagine if you could bring the very best ideas and effort out of your team each and every day. What if you could create a company that organically attracted amazing talent? And what if it wasn't all on you, as a leader, to make this happen?

Not only would the company grow more quickly, but it would grow more easily.

Not only would it be easier for you to lead, but it would be more fun.

You'd build a company that matters. A company that you're proud of.

As you'll soon see, the process is quite simple.

But first we need to understand why so many companies fall into this trap—over and over again—of becoming yet another mediocre company.

THE CULTURE-BUILDING DILEMMA

Most founders and leaders know that culture is important, but early stage businesses are demanding. There's always a new milestone

THE JOURNEY OF BUILDING A COMPANY DOESN'T HAPPEN IN A STRAIGHT LINE.

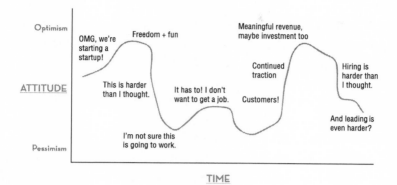

that needs to be prioritized. A key hire to fill out the leadership team. The next round to raise. An important customer to close. The next feature to ship.

Culture gets put on the back burner and becomes a "nice-to-have," while business-building remains the "must-have."

For some founders, it's easy to neglect being deliberate about culture because everything is going great. You may have a small team with strong bonds that were forged in the early fire of getting the company off the ground and well-chosen newcomers picking up on the vibe by osmosis. When things are going well early on, it can be hard to see the value of investing in culture. You may even feel that you're prematurely becoming too corporate and fear that something might be lost or made to feel inorganic by focusing on culture.

Most leaders wait to start attending to company culture until they have hired a full-time, senior-level leader or HR person. This usually occurs when the headcount is between 50 and 150, but by then much of the culture has already solidified without any intentionality around how it was created.

This pattern is so common that we've named the phenomena the Culture-Building Dilemma.

The Culture-Building Dilemma Is Simply This:

- In the early days of building a business and raising money, most founders and leaders—even the ones who acknowledge the importance of culture—prioritize the business and money over culture.
- They think to themselves, *I'll pay attention to culture when we are big enough, stable enough, have enough mental bandwidth to deal with it, have the right person to do that...*
- But by the time they get "big enough" or "stable enough," a default culture has already been established. For teams that raise capital, this happens even more quickly as the pressure to grow and succeed gets dialed up even higher.
- Leaders are left scrambling to keep the wheels on as the business begins to scale.
- In the midst of the chaos, well-intentioned leaders hope that tending to culture might mitigate the chaos, so they make a mild, half-hearted attempt at culture-building. Some form of company values is quickly assembled and explained to the team in the hopes that it'll create some significant course correction or shift.
- But the effort has no lasting impact on the actual culture. It was too little, too late.
- The end result is another mediocre company. And what a shame; the company once had so much promise, so much potential. A chance to be different. To be special. To be unique. To be a place where people loved their work because the work mattered.

The world is riddled with companies like this. You've probably worked at one. These types of companies struggle to create a positive work environment. They compromise their true values. And they fail to take care of their employees.

The business suffers, experiencing lower productivity, slower innovation, high employee turnover, unsustainable stress, and smaller profit margins.

The people miss out on an opportunity to be a part of something bigger, something truly special. And the leaders lose a chance to build something that matters, something they're proud to have created.

But, as a leader, you have a choice: To make culture a priority. To be different. To be unique. To be special. To build an iconic company that leaves a lasting, positive impression on everyone you touch.

We believe that the world already has enough mediocre companies. If you're holding this book, then you probably feel the same.

We don't want to sugarcoat things here; intentionally designing and building your company's culture takes real work and dedication. This isn't a one-time project. There is no shortcut or hack. The work won't always be easy, but as you'll see, it is straightforward.

And we're here to help guide the way.

In your hands, you're holding a proven playbook for designing a vibrant, unique, and iconic company culture. The process that we'll walk you through was created and refined through our own hard-won experience.

One of us has spent the last 25 years consulting and coaching leaders at over two hundred companies, including Slack, Twitter, Coursera, Dropbox, Tile, Eero, Bandcamp, and Cricket Health. The other has been a founder at multiple companies, raised venture capital, and scaled teams and along the way wished for a practical and proven guide to startup culture. This book is that guide: a culmination of years of our experience and effort in building healthy, effective startup cultures. If you'd like to know more about either of us, we've included more detailed bios at the end of the book.

The chapters ahead are an invitation for you to make explicit what matters most as you build your company, and by doing so, to bring a new level of intentionality to building a culture and a company that you are proud of.

We're going to walk you step-by-step through designing and building your culture. We call this approach the *Culture-Building Roadmap*.

THE CULTURE-BUILDING ROADMAP

The *Culture-Building Roadmap* is a proven approach for creating and building a company that you are proud of and that attracts the best and the brightest—a company that you yourself would want to work for—without taking your eye off the business.

Here's what you need to do now—before it's too late—to have a chance at creating a company culture that you would want to work for.

These are the six steps we're going to walk you through:

1. **Discover:** Your team and company already has a culture, an essence that is implicit to who you are and how you work. We'll begin by getting curious about that essence and, through a series of conversations, making your implicit culture explicit. This creates the foundation to build upon.

2. **Design:** After discovering your unique essence, we'll use those insights to create a first version of your Culture Code that is authentic, energizing, succinct, and useful for clarifying what matters most.

3. **Prototype:** Then, before rushing your Culture Code out the door, we'll test it within your leadership team in a live prototype. By activating your Culture Code as daily practice and setting up a regular feedback loop, you'll refine your Culture Code within your team until it's proven to be ready.

4. **Embed:** Once your Culture Code is proven by your proto-

type, we'll put it into action. We'll show you exactly how to embed culture in all three dimensions of your company. The day-to-day functioning of your company will reinforce and celebrate your culture throughout your team's processes, rituals, and communication.

5. **Amplify:** Here we seek to increase the quantity of culture-builders in your organization so ongoing culture-building is everyone's shared responsibility. By training people in how to create "culture-in-action" moments every day, you'll create an environment and expectation that everyone is a culture-builder.

6. **Iterate:** Culture-building, like product-building, never ends. We'll show you how to run new culture-building experiments to constantly test, gather feedback, learn new things, and improve your culture's effectiveness.

WHAT THIS BOOK WILL TEACH YOU

In the coming pages, we're going to teach you everything that you need to know to design a great company culture—one that creates a powerful connectedness in your team, improves performance, and helps cultivate a company vibe that attracts others.

This includes:

- Exactly how to get started designing your culture
- How to enroll your leadership team in the entire process
- When to begin inviting others at the company to join the process
- How to capture and communicate what matters most so everyone in your organization is 100 percent aligned
- A method for documenting a Culture Code that is uniquely yours, energizes your team, and is simple for all to understand

- How to name and communicate your Culture Code so it feels completely authentic
- Ways that you can bring your Culture Code alive in the day-to-day work so people experience and appreciate it every day
- An approach for rolling out your Culture Code to your team that makes everyone feel bought-in and feel a real sense of ownership
- How to continually learn about, refine, and improve your culture over time

Along the way, we'll also reveal insider stories and examples that bring to life the journey that leaders take as they build culture. To make these stories as straightforward as possible, we've elected to share them from a collective ("we") perspective, even though in some cases the examples come from just one of the authors' client or leadership experiences. Again, our goal is to create the clearest picture that we can to help you build your own culture.

Our aim is to give you everything that you might need for this process. At the end of the book you will find further resources for each of the steps and a way of contacting us if you would like to engage additional culture-building support.

WHAT THIS BOOK WON'T TEACH YOU

We also want to be clear on what this book isn't, so you know what you're not getting:

- This book is not a quick shortcut. Building culture requires real effort. Any quick fix or "do this and you're done" approaches aren't real. We will, however, help you use your time for maximum efficiency and impact.
- You aren't going to learn any theory of culture here. There's

intentionally no fluff or high-level concepts to grasp. This book is grounded in proven, actionable advice.

* This book isn't a guaranteed way to create the exact company that you want. We'll give you the building blocks that we've seen create the conditions for success in scaling without losing your soul. But ultimately, culture is built in daily interactions with people. You can follow every piece of our advice and yet undermine everything if your behaviors aren't in alignment. This book doesn't get you out of needing to show up for your team each and every day.

CULTURE-BUILDING ROADMAP
A Proven Approach for Building a Company You Are Proud Of

1 DISCOVER
Discover the living, breathing cultural essence that your team and company already has.

2 DESIGN
Design a Culture Code that is authentic, energizing, succinct, behaviorally explicit, and brand-reinforcing.

3 PROTOTYPE
Prototype living your culture within your leadership before rushing your Culture Code out the door.

4 EMBED
Embed your Culture Code throughout the organization: people processes, meeting rituals, decision-making, and the look & feel of your brand.

5 AMPLIFY
Amplify your desired culture by increasing the number of people acting as culture-builders in your company.

6 ITERATE
Iterate by deciding on the metrics you will use to track progress and continually improve. Culture-building, like product building, never ends.

HOW TO USE THIS BOOK

We recommend starting with a quick read through the entire book. This will help you understand where we're headed, while also giving you a picture of how all six of the steps will build upon each other.

While the *Culture-Building Roadmap* is entirely doable by a single person, if you have an intact leadership or executive team or co-founders at the business, we encourage tackling these steps together as a group. Involving others early creates accountability and broadens perspectives as you go. If you're not sure who to involve just yet, that's okay. Read ahead and you'll get a clearer picture of who you want to involve at the different stages of the process.

After completing a first read-through, you can then use each chapter as a step-by-step guide for your own culture-building process.

When you're ready, let's get started.

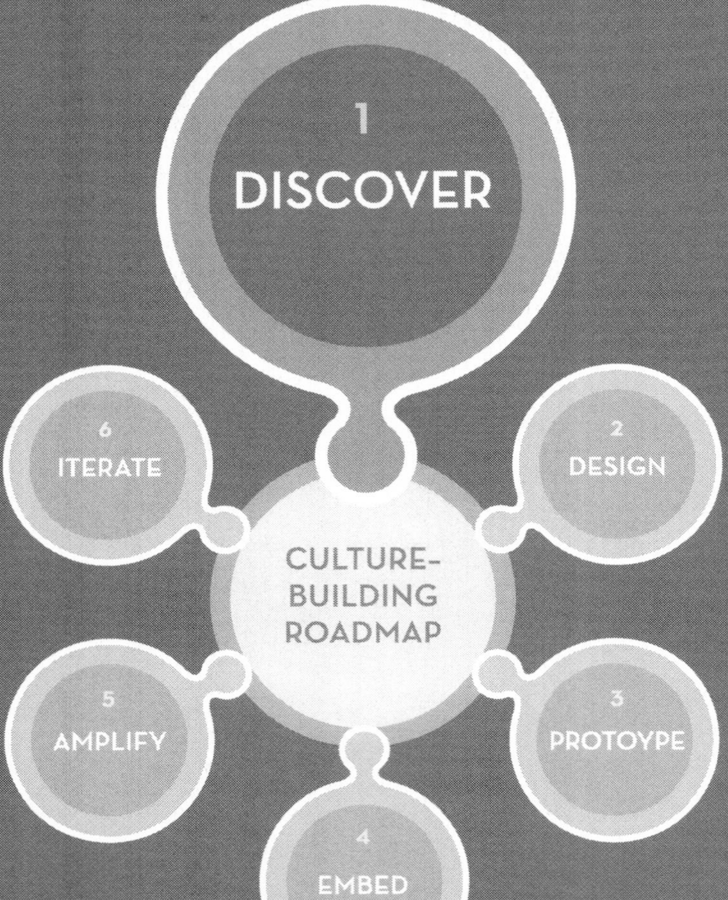

CULTURE-
BUILDING
ROADMAP

1 DISCOVER

2 DESIGN

3 PROTOYPE

4 EMBED

5 AMPLIFY

6 ITERATE

DISCOVER

Your company already has
an essence. What is it?

Most company founders and leaders that we work with already know that their company culture matters. They know culture influences everything. They know it's important to get it right. And they know that it can be a true competitive advantage.

But when they first start working on their culture, they encounter a common pitfall: they treat culture as a thing or set of things *to do*. This line of thinking turns culture into an item to check off the list so that they can get back to business. The thinking goes, "If we *do* x, y, and z, then we will *have* the culture we want."

This check-the-box approach to "doing culture" doesn't work and doesn't scale. It generally follows one of two predictable paths:

1. The "Ping-Pong, PR, and Perks Culture"

Inspired by some of the early culture innovators (Google being a prime example), founders try to create a fun environment for work. On the back of their latest fundraise, they invest in a cool headquarters, usually with brightly colored walls, witty wall hangings, and free lunches or happy hours. Everyone gets "unlimited" vacation and a company hoodie. Leadership hopes that this generates positive PR, translates into engagement within the company, and earns them a good enough reputation to attract the talent they need.

But this approach leaves you with nothing special about your company beyond the perks—and perks aren't unique. On this path, you create an endless game of needing to out-perk other companies. Eventually, when the fun fades—and it will—you're left with a hollow, soulless business.

2. The "Hustle Culture"

Phrases like "We just get shit done," "We hire doers," and "We move fast and break things" are commonplace. Each is a rallying cry to work more, work harder, and work faster. Hustle culture manufactures a collective pride around being fully committed. This sets up a slippery slope by prioritizing productivity over people. Long hours become expected, all in the name of squeezing out the maximum effectiveness from each and every employee.

Admittedly, sometimes this approach works well in the early days. It can help you assemble an A-team of high performers, but with scale comes challenges. Burnout is always lurking around the corner, accompanied by an almost guaranteed low emotional intelligence culture.

And honestly, many teams have a combination of the above approaches.

The problem with these approaches is that they result in an endless cycle of needing to keep doing the next thing in an effort to keep people happy and engaged. There's no deeper meaning than perks and/or working hard. You'll never arrive at a great team culture this way. Trying to *do* culture results in a watered-down, derivative culture that's often a cookie-cutter imitation of other companies' cultures.

Great cultures attract the best talent and bring the best out of people because they have a certain vibe to them that results from deeper shared meaning. It's not about *do*-ing; it's a way of *be*-ing. You can feel it when you enter the room. It's the difference between walking into a party where the group is really in sync and connected with each other versus a party where the mood seems awkward and conversations feel forced and contrived.

You can't fake, force, or copy a vibe. You're going to need to foster your own from the ingredients you have at hand. The good news is that the beginnings already exist. Your team already has a unique culture—an "essence" that can be uncovered. Your job is to get curious about what it is, in order to more fully discover it.

WHAT IS YOUR COMPANY'S ESSENCE?

Just as each person has a unique essence, each company has an essence, an identity, a soul, a distinct DNA that is uniquely its own. When we say "essence," we're pointing at a way of being that includes and transcends your purpose, implicit beliefs, and values.

This essence or "way of being" has a look, sound, and feel to it. It resonates with some qualities more than others. These qualities of being are what you're aiming to discover. Your company's essence is more than just a list of values. Or a purpose statement. Or some desired behaviors. It is what animates all of those things and ties them together.

In discovering your company's essence, you will encounter strengths, weaknesses, shadows, and untapped resources. Once it's distinguished and articulated, it can become a powerful vitalizing force for your company. This process will help you to carry the best of your existing company culture into the future while leaving what isn't working behind.

THINK LIKE AN ANTHROPOLOGIST

Think of yourself as an anthropologist who has traveled to a faraway, foreign place called *(insert-the-name-of-your-company-here)* Land. You are the first outsider to visit this place. Your mission is to understand without bias as much as you can about the people and culture of this new place.

As you observe the inhabitants of this place, see how many distinct cultural phenomena you can notice. Pay attention to everything from how people behave and communicate, to where and when they gather, to how they deal with setbacks and success. How do they welcome new people? How do they say goodbye to those who leave? Notice the daily and weekly rituals used for problem-solving and celebrations, the quality of the listening in daily interactions. Are people heads down most of the time? What's the emotional tone in the room? What are the symbols and the characteristics of the physical space, and how do people move within the space? Do they get upset about certain things? Do they avoid certain topics? Notice whether some people have more power than others, which may correlate with the roles they have, but not always.

All of these factors can help *point* to your company's implicit culture and essence.

DISCOVERING YOUR ESSENCE USING APPRECIATIVE INQUIRY

This first step is all about unearthing the essence of the organization through exploratory conversations with the founders, the leaders, and the team. You're looking for a clear answer to questions like: What is the cultural DNA of our company? What makes us distinct and uniquely us?

To find the answers, we use a process based on a framework known as Appreciative Inquiry.[1] It's a framework that begins by assuming that a "positive core" already exists (on your team, in your company). Renaissance sculptor Michelangelo said, "Every block of stone has a statue inside it and it is the task of the sculptor to discover it." When creating the *David*, he began with the belief that David was already inside the block of marble, and his job was simply removing all of the pieces that weren't part of him.

Your company also already has a wonderful core essence. There's nothing that you need to create. You just need to uncover what's already there.

With this mindset in place, Appreciative Inquiry uses open-ended questions to focus attention on *existing values, capacities, strengths*, and *successes* to discover your essence.

---

1   Developed by David Cooperrider and Suresh Srivastva at Case Western Reserve University.

For Early Stage Startups: Begin with Yourself

If your company is at an early stage (fewer than ten people), start by reflecting on what you're already bringing to your company's culture, both consciously and unconsciously.

The essence of a company is always heavily impacted by its founders and early leadership, so not only will capturing your impressions yield valuable information, but surfacing your thoughts now will free you up in the coming steps to focus more on what others have to share.

Start by spending fifteen to twenty minutes writing answers to the following:

- What led you to found (or join) the company?
- What were your hopes for the company's impact?
- How did you envision the team working together? And how do you actually work together?
- What have been the very best moments of the work so far? What about those moments was especially impactful to you?

Notice the words, phrases, and sentiments that feel the most compelling to you. After you have captured your own thoughts, you're ready to engage the rest of your team.

DISCOVERING YOUR ESSENCE WITH YOUR LEADERSHIP TEAM

Gather your leadership team for a ninety-minute culture discovery working session.

Introduce the meeting by setting the context: this time is solely for brainstorming and discussing the unique characteristics of your culture. You're not here to make any decisions, just to explore.

If the meeting is in-person, each person will need twenty to forty Post-it notes and a Sharpie marker. You'll also want a whiteboard or flipchart for organizing the notes.

If your team is meeting virtually, we suggest using a virtual whiteboard like Whimsical, Mural, or Miro to organize your work together.

Running the Meeting

Step 1: Start with five to ten minutes of independent brainstorming in which each person answers the following prompts:

* What is distinctive, unique, or iconic about this team and our company?
* What are a few of our most notable, memorable, or impact-ful stories as a company? What do these stories say about the kind of company we are?
* How do we treat each other when we are at our best?
* Who is most effective in their work here? What characteristics enable their success and impact?

Each new answer or thought should get its own Post-it note.

Step 2: Give each person a turn to bring their Post-its to the whiteboard. Have them read each Post-it out loud and then place it on the whiteboard.

If an idea that is shared is unclear to anyone in the room, it should be clarified and possibly rewritten right away.

As topics are shared, group similar ideas near one another. For example, a story about *that time when a developer fixed a critical bug without being asked to* might be grouped with another Post-it that mentions that the *team is most effective when everyone has a large amount of autonomy.*

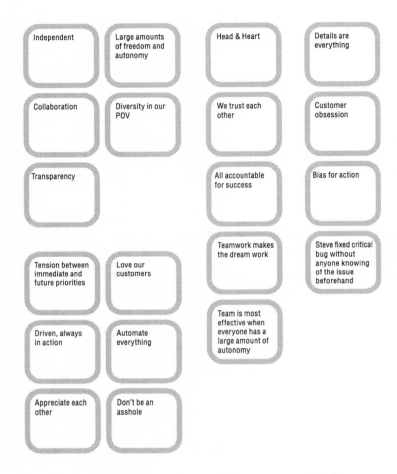

Example of what a first set of Post-its might look like

Don't worry about being too precise with groupings. If they're related in some way, put them near each other and call that good enough. The groupings exist only to make the next step, a group discussion, easier.

You can make this process even more powerful by having people snap or softly clap when someone shares an idea that they agree with

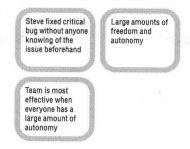

Example of a quick grouping as you read out ideas

but might not have written down themselves. This starts to build energy around topics that are most likely to hold important insights.

Step 3: Once everyone has had a chance to share, spend the remaining time (usually forty-five minutes to an hour) discussing what's been captured on the whiteboard.

To help guide your discussion:

- Ask the group, "What here has the most energy behind it for you?" Explore their answers further together.
- Are there topics that most everyone mentioned? Talk more about the truth and impact behind those topics.
- As new stories and ideas surface, add them to the whiteboard.
- If a clear theme has surfaced, consider giving it a name on the whiteboard (e.g., "Autonomy," "Caring for Our Customers," "Working as a Team"). In doing this, remember to focus more on capturing the essence of what is true about your team and less on the actual words that you use. Finding the precise language to communicate your essence comes next.

At the conclusion of the meeting, thank everyone for sharing and capturing everything from the whiteboard. Take photos or screen-

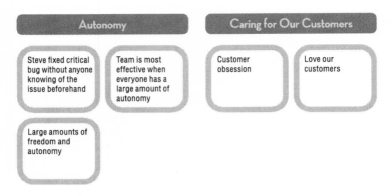

Examples of themes beginning to emerge

shots of the whiteboard and have someone agree to get the notes transcribed into a shared location. For many teams, a shared document or spreadsheet is fine for this process. We've also encountered a handful of tools that can help facilitate and capture this process for both remote and in-person teams, which you can find in the Resources section at www.scalewithoutlosingyoursoul.com.

WHAT IF WE'VE ALREADY CREATED COMPANY VALUES BEFORE?

Many teams have already created some version of their core values when we first meet them. Often the values were drafted with good intentions, but not much changed after they were created.

One leadership team that we worked with had created a three-page document listing their values and uploaded it to their internal wiki about a year before we met them. Hardly anyone had looked at it since. Another team had realized that the first draft of their values was far too aspirational. They had painted a picture that simply wasn't who they were, which created some level of disillusion within the company.

We also encounter teams who sense that they've simply outgrown or are unsure of their currently drafted values.

Whatever the situation, the key question to ask is: How confident am I that our current values accurately capture our company's essence?

If you're anything less than 100 percent confident here, you should work through the entire Discover step. In doing so, you'll use your current values as important information in the data that you collect. But don't let them bias the discovery process. Take extra care to use open-ended questions during surveys, focus groups, and interviews to help surface new insights. This approach ensures that the data that you gather either affirms or brings into question what was previously drafted.

By starting the discovery process with a blank slate, that team with the three-page document on their wiki found that several of their previously stated values simply weren't true and that the resulting incongruence had cast doubt over the entire list. Situations like this are incredibly common, and this is exactly why rediscovering who you really are is worth the effort.

LEVERAGING YOUR ENTIRE ORGANIZATION TO DISCOVER YOUR ESSENCE

You may also want to tap into the wisdom of the entire organization to discover your essence, especially if a large portion of your team isn't on the leadership team. By doing so, you will surface new insights into your company's essential nature, including things that might be blind spots to you and your leadership team.

When engaging the broader team, select someone (either internal or external) to conduct an Appreciative Inquiry process—via surveys, interviews, focus groups, and/or direct observation—that elicits the defining stories and themes of your company's essence.

Here are a handful of helpful ways to help get the most useful information from your team:

1. **Clearly frame the process for others:** Help put everyone who engages in the process at ease by explaining that this is nothing more than an exploration, that their responses will be held anonymously (or confidentially, if in a focus group), and that they're encouraged to be as honest as possible.

2. **Engage both sides of the brain:** Aim to engage people in both their left brain (words, phrases, qualities) and their right brain (stories about feelings, symbols, inside jokes, etc.).

3. **Aim to surface stories:** Ask broad, open-ended questions to evoke spontaneous responses and stories. These are a few of our favorite questions:
   > What are some of the most impactful, memorable, or notable stories at our company?
   > Who are examples of notable or important people here and what qualities do they have?
   > What are some examples of us at our best?

4. **Spot opportunities to go deeper:** During live interviews or focus groups, when you get a response that makes you curious, use follow-up questions to go a bit deeper. You'll be surprised by how a follow-up question as simple as "What does that tell you about the kind of company we are?" can create an entirely new and valuable insight.

5. **Learn unique information from new employees:** While newer team members won't have a history of stories from their work to tap, their first impressions can reveal a lot. Consider using different questions for newer employees:
   > What was it about this company that convinced you to work here?
   > What most stood out to you during your interview/hiring process?
   > What is most different about working here versus other places you've worked?

WHERE THERE IS LIGHT, THERE IS SHADOW

"One does not become enlightened by imagining figures of light, but by making the darkness conscious."
—C. G. Jung

Exploring the positive core of your company is important, but it's only half the story. Once you've uncovered numerous examples of essential qualities and values present within your team and larger company, it's important to also look for and discover the behaviors/trends/processes/systems that exist but may be in opposition to your stated or aspired-to values and culture.

These are your organizational shadows. They are topics that are generally not discussed openly and are often intentionally hidden. Organizational shadows are unavoidable, and good culture does not mean absence of shadow. In a sense, the specific shadow elements within your team or company are a consequence of the kind of culture you choose to create. Every group of people has elements that are contrary to who they aspire to be. The important thing is to be able to see them and talk about them.

Matt Auron, co-founder and managing director of Evolution, shares more on the phenomenon of shadow:

Organizations are merely groups of people working together to complete tasks, so shadows can exist there too, in the collective. These covert processes are the coalitions, secret alliances, and counter-values that guide sometimes bad behavior and can have disastrous impacts. Shadow much of the time is the exact counterbalance of what is espoused. Relationship- and community-based culture? Surely lurking beneath the surface is individualistic or cutthroat competitiveness. Value of customer service first? Usually it is easy to find corners cut to ensure costs are controlled.[2]

The best culture discovery processes focus on both the essence *and* the shadow—either on the same day or sequentially within a specific time period. When we invite a group to talk about some of the shadow elements of their culture, we encourage them to be direct and honest but also constructive. The goal of this conversation is to surface some of these themes without blaming or criticizing anyone. This is not a complaining session but rather an opportunity to generate more data so we can identify the systems, processes, and values to put in place to help make the company better.

The process is similar to the one for discovering essence but with different prompts:

- Where are we misaligned with who we say we are as an organization?
- Where are there tensions between different aspects of our work?

---

2   Auron, Matt. "The Shadow Side of Organizational Culture." Medium, February 6, 2017. https://medium.com/@mattauron/the-shadow-side-of-organizational -culture-907f316445e6.

- What are some aspects of our culture that aren't working?
- What is undiscussed or hidden about who we are?

It often helps to have a third-party facilitator for this part who can help draw the group out and translate what they are hearing into accurate yet neutral words and phrases that will be useful later. For example, here are some of the themes from a recent culture discovery day:

TOP 10 - GREEN GROUP

ESSENCE	Shadows
1 Transparency	1 Speed over quality
2 Inclusively cliquish	2 Unrealistic expectations
3 Humaness/empathy	3 Role + reporting ambiguity
4 Empowered to succeed	4 Silo'd / lack of x-fredng
5 Working It - whatever it takes	5 Can't say no
6 Open + sincere gratitude	6 Lack of flow time
7 Powerfully ambitious	7 Unsustainable pace that leads to burnout
8 Practical innovation	8 Failures aren't openly addressed
9 Strategic + Practical	9 Spread too thin
10 Sharpen before you cut	10 Work-life balance confusion. work = life?

Capturing these themes helped open up a good conversation about work/life balance, as well as a need for more cross-functional teaming versus loyalty to one's own team. It also directly helped shape one of the principles in the final Culture Code: "Speak Up and Move Forward." This principle encouraged folks to both pro-actively share context and be transparent about needs with other teams, while also tending to the need for alignment and speed.

Unfortunately, most founders shy away from this part of the process, and as a result, their culture-building efforts don't gain the traction they'd hoped for. In an earnest effort to create a better culture, these founders and leaders tend to focus on the positive side and ignore the shadow side. But if we can't talk about it, we can't learn from it, and we can't attend to it.

HOW CASTLIGHT AND COURSERA ENGAGED THEIR WHOLE COMPANIES

Castlight Health, a health-tech company making it easier for people to navigate the health system, hired us to train a team of cross-functional leaders to be their culture champions. These motivated leaders got on the same page about how to define and talk about company culture and how to facilitate the discovery process. They then led four hundred people through a series of asynchronous focus groups on essence and shadow, and aggregated the themes that emerged. Then the exec team did a gut check to identify their unique essence. A few weeks later, the COO presented the Culture Code and had one culture champion tell a story for each identified value.

During Coursera's culture process, the company shut down the business for a day to do their culture discovery. It started with a Culture 101 talk introducing why their time investment was worth it, followed by an overview of the rest of the day. The entire team was then split into breakout groups facilitated by different leaders who had been trained in advance on how to elicit essence and shadow themes. They ended the day with an all-company celebration. Over the next two weeks, the input was gathered and distilled into Coursera's values and was brought back to the larger group in another all-company meeting.

In both of these examples, providing a shared context around culture was important. It helped everyone buy into the process. Also, having senior leaders out in front, leading the discovery process, added credibility to the whole effort.

HOW ONE CEO INVITED EVERYONE TO PARTICIPATE IN THE DISCOVERY PROCESS

Below is an actual email sent by a venture-backed CEO inviting their team into the discovery process. Feel free to use and adapt this for your own culture process.

Hi team,

Our culture at [our company] is the foundation of how we work together—how we interact with each other, how we learn and improve, and how we creatively build and scale our business.

As we grow as a team, I believe it is becoming increasingly important to crystallize our culture, capture the awesome parts of who we are as well as the things we still want to work on and improve.

In pursuit of that goal, we are launching our company culture project today. This is a unique opportunity for everyone to take an active part in defining our culture as we continue to scale.

To help us in this process we have engaged Simon D'Arcy and Todd Emaus at Evolution—a firm that specializes in helping startups like ours to "scale without losing their soul." They have *helped some of the fastest growing companies around including Slack, Snapchat, Coursera, and others. Simon facilitated our last exec team off-site and led us through a similar process on a smaller scale—we believe he's really good at what he does and can help us tremendously in this process.*

The first step in the process will be a company-wide survey to help clarify our essence by asking "What makes [our company] iconic, distinct, and/or unique?" We want to hear as many specific examples from as many people as possible. I would like to ask for your engagement and participation in order to make this process as significant as possible.

>>>Take the survey HERE<<<

As always, feel free to write to me with any questions or feedback you might have.

Best,

CEO

YOUR TURN: DISCOVER YOUR COMPANY'S ESSENCE

As they say in the world of Appreciative Inquiry, "In every human system, something works." The Discover step is about uncovering what's already working for you and beginning to find the words that best describe those traits, characteristics, and flavors of your company's essence. For most of our clients, the very act of spending group time and attention focused on this becomes a memorable culture-building moment in and of itself.

By taking the time to discover your company's essence, you unearth the deeper truth of who you are and what matters most to you. You'll gather all sorts of information that will be the material that you'll be working with as you move into the next step: Design.

CHECKLIST FOR THE DISCOVER STEP

This step is about embracing culture as a way of being and not just as things that you do. Your way of being begins with discovering your company's deeper essence: the unique beliefs, attitudes, and mindsets that are vital to who you are as a group.

During the Discover step:
- ☐ Use Appreciative Inquiry to understand your essence as a company by exploring:
  - · Meaningful moments from the past
  - · Notable employees and what it was that set them apart
  - · What makes your company unique from others
  - · The behaviors or qualities that you exhibit when you're at your best
- ☐ Work through individual journaling, conversations with your leadership team, and focus groups with your team as methods for surfacing information.
- ☐ Identify and discuss shadows in your organization that might undermine the culture that you intend to build.
- ☐ Capture everything notable that surfaces during these conversations in a single location. A Google Sheet or something similar is perfect.

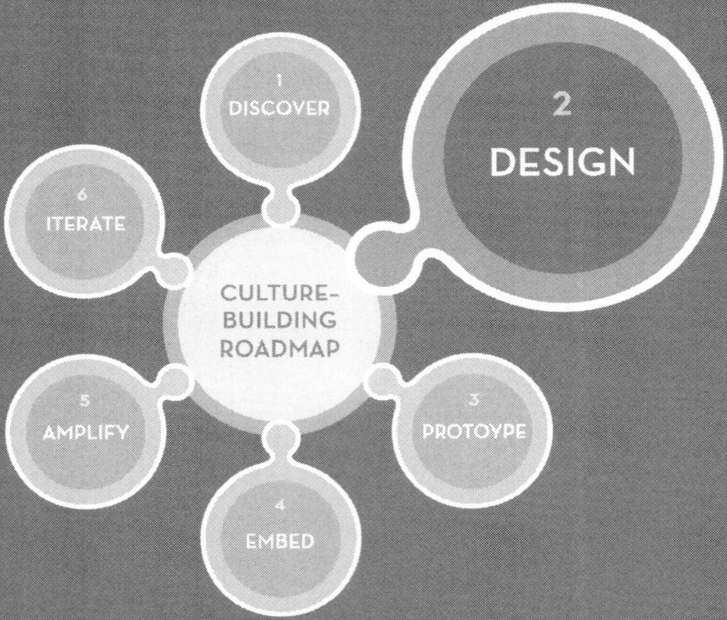

CULTURE-
BUILDING
ROADMAP

1
DISCOVER

2
DESIGN

3
PROTOYPE

4
EMBED

5
AMPLIFY

6
ITERATE

STEP 2

DESIGN

Crafting your Culture Code.

Most companies never take the time to draft their core values. Those that do tend to scramble to hammer them out quickly. In a rush to get back to work, they'll come up with a list of values filled with corporate-sounding clichés, wishful thinking, and emotionless phrases. The end result is a forgotten list of words or, worse, the values become evidence for skeptics.

Of course there are positive intentions behind these efforts to create a list of aspirational values that make the company look good to the public. But this approach fails to acknowledge the existing essence of the team and company. And while a list of values may look good on paper, these values aren't lived out within the organization. This never plays out well over time, as employees grow disillusioned with the organization's inauthenticity. Underperformance and employee churn result.

Other well-meaning companies struggle to craft a Culture Code that accurately captures their essence. One company that we worked with—a financial services firm—had made a commitment early on to prioritize culture. The founders had been partners at one of the big consulting firms and vowed to create a different sort of workplace. The CEO even went by the unofficial title of "Keeper of the Culture." But their commitment had led them down a path of over-definition. They had ten core values—a lot for anyone to recall or internalize. But that's not all. They also had a supplemental list of behavioral expectations (the do's and don'ts of the company). There were nine of these, and many overlapped with the values, only phrased differently. Unsurprisingly, when a random manager or employee was asked what the company's values were, they were able to name only a select few items, which were often a mix from both lists.

In the Design step, we take the insights from the Discover step and turn them into a first draft of your company's Culture Code that meets four distinct criteria that set you and your organization up for the future.

FROM ESSENCE TO CULTURE CODE

In the same way that your biological DNA defines your physical traits, tendencies, and aptitudes, your organization has a DNA that influences how people behave, collaborate, and achieve results. A Culture Code simply captures that DNA and acts as a singular source of truth for your company's beliefs and values. It becomes one of your core defining documents, alongside other company-defining materials, like your mission, vision, organizational structure, and/ or leadership principles.

Some companies create an elaborate Culture Code that spans multiple pages in a beautifully designed employee handbook. Other companies have a one-page document that clearly defines the mission, vision, and values of the organization. Some teams prefer images over words. The only rule to follow in creating a Culture Code is to *make sure that it is uniquely yours.*

Think of your Culture Code as a blueprint for the type of organization you're building.

As you design your Culture Code, there are four criteria to aim for:

1. **Authentically yours.** Good Culture Codes are unique to you and you alone. No one could ever copy it.
2. **Powerfully energizing.** There needs to be a certain spark to the words—a challenge to be your very best, a possibility to make the impact that you want, and a desire to fully live it. You, your team, and those considering joining your mission should all feel it.
3. **Succinct.** Short. Easily memorable. No fluff, no filler. Every component has a purpose.
4. **Clarifying.** It should empower your team to make quicker decisions while they do the best work of their life.

Great Culture Codes capture your organization's DNA, which carries within it the code that defines the character and proficiency of the entire organism. By codifying your culture in words, it becomes easier to talk about, embed, amplify, and scale as your company grows.

A well-designed Culture Code becomes an invitation to bring your finest self to your work. It describes the best parts of a culture that already exists while also being a declaration of an even better possible future.

Culture Codes can go by all sorts of names, such as core values, founding principles, or manifestos. We use "Culture Code" because in the same way that software code guides a computer in how to operate, your Culture Code guides your team in how to behave as you work together. Marketing software maker HubSpot also uses "Culture Code," saying that it is "the operating system that powers HubSpot."[3]

If "Culture Code" doesn't feel right to you, we'll help you find the name that's a better fit for you and your team in the coming steps.

HOW TO CREATE YOUR CULTURE CODE

Begin by answering the question: From all of the quotes and stories shared, what are the most distinctive themes that emerged?

Take all of the data from the Discover step and begin organizing it into themes. Open up a spreadsheet (Excel or Google Sheets is fine) or a drag-and-drop sticky note tool (Whimsical is one of our favorites) and start combining related thoughts into themed groups or buckets.

Within each theme, pull out some of the main ideas into a headline of sorts. The headline might be a short sentence or a series of phrases/words that make the theme easy to identify in ongoing conversations.

---

3   Shah, Dharmesh. "The HubSpot Culture Code." HubSpot, June 24, 2021. https://network.hubspot.com/slides/the-hubspot-culture-code-1f8v2ot3a?p=2.

People / Generosity / Empathy / Family / Community / Fun / Supportive

Annual family day, everyone is close

Kindness is a quality that most of us possess in a big way

Lots of positive energy, saying hello to people, engaging, humor

Comfortable with each other, forgetting about working relationship

People are acknowledged (ex. #thanks channel)

Pioneering / Cutting Edge / Exploration / Going Above and Beyond

Always looking to find a path and embrace new problems

We love mind-blowing technology and want to be the best at what we do

We're pioneers, embracing the crazy ideas

When I was interviewing here, I noticed the team had a sense of wonder and they lit up when talking about tasks, even challenges—it sold me on joining

Organized chaos— very experimental, make decisions on the go, and then figure out if they were smart ones

Stepping Up / Pitching In / Persistence / Coming Together

Coming together as a team when needed (ex. Buzz project)

Stick-to-itiveness and problem-solving —no matter how big the tech challenge or how impossible a task, there's a sense we can get it done

Willingness to pitch in

Dogged persistence, seeing things through, going all the way, hustling to make the impossible possible

Autonomy / Ownership (of the vision) / Trusting / Not Micromanaging

Autonomy: I feel trusted, and there's no micromanagement

Trusting even the newest employee to tackle a big problem: autonomy, ownership

It's possible to run with an idea and be trusted to make something of it

Don't overthink things. Often a good headline is in the comments gathered from the Discover step and is staring you right in the face. When naming a headline elicits distinctive ideas, then it's time to zoom out. You likely have more than a single idea inside the bucket. Split the ideas into separate buckets for now.

To give you an idea of what your theming might look like, here is an actual theme summary we helped create:

Here is a similar example from another company:

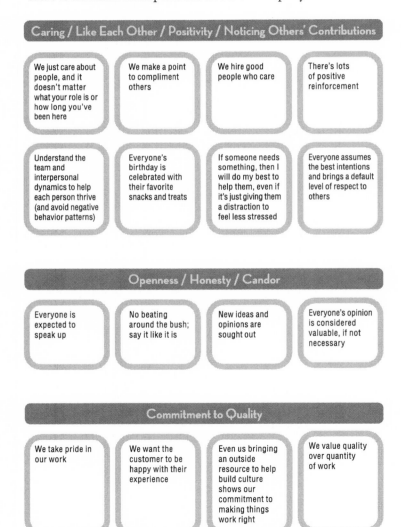

We All Do Our Part / Autonomy / Team Mentality

I want to help the team, not for my own success but our success	We all trust each other to get our things done	We don't shy away from hard work nor the hard questions	We all roll up our sleeves
Nothing is beneath anyone	I feel responsible for my projects but know others can and will help	We all want to get it done, and we will get it done	I feel invested in our success—both as a group and in each individual

Committed to Best Ideas Winning / Strong Opinions

We want strong opinions loosely held	We are committed to finding the best answer (e.g., confrontational debate across multiple viewpoints with rationale, not ego)	Strong opinions are constantly updated

Always Learning / Experimentation

We state hypotheses and then test them	Mistakes are good if you learn from them	Nothing is sacred; question everything

In this example, you'll notice that the theme of "Caring for Each Other / Positivity / Noticing Others' Contributions" includes quotes and stories captured during focus groups:

- "We just care about people and it doesn't matter what your role is or how long you've been here. We care."

- "There's lots of positive reinforcement."
- Everyone's birthday is celebrated with their favorite snacks and treats.

Another theme, "We All Do Our Part / Autonomy / Team Mentality," **came from** bucketing the following together:

- "I want to help the team. Not for my own success but our success."
- "We all trust each other to get our things done."
- A story that was shared about feeling responsible for individual projects but knowing others can and will help.

With each grouping, you're distilling a set of ideas, quotes, and stories into the clear themes that are emerging.

THEME CONSOLIDATION

Take all the notes beneath each headline and boil them down to a few quotes and/or bullet points that accurately describe the theme. What are the 1–3 quotes or stories that best express the essence of this theme?

In this step, you're making each theme easier to understand and easier to talk about through the remainder of the design process.

Be sure to preserve and pull through the character of the comments. It's important not to lose the metaphors, unique language, and iconic references or stories that give your Culture Code an authentic feel. Keep these when you can.

In talking with one team during their discovery process, there were a variety of stories shared about the importance of empowering each other and being able to move quickly and make decisions, while also trusting that even in the instances where something went sideways, there was still a belief that the person responsible was doing their best.

At this point, the theme might look something like the following:

After consolidating each theme into a few quotes, you will often have more clarity on what certain themes are really about. Consider which headlines might benefit from being updated now that you've consolidated. Craft better headlines wherever you see the opportunity.

WHAT TO DO WITH YOUR SHADOW THEMES

Shadow themes usually fall into one of two categories: feedback to become curious about or a polarity to attend to.

How to Use Shadow Themes as Feedback

You can tell what matters to someone by listening to what they complain about.

Some of what you hear in your shadow sessions might be familiar, and some of it will likely be new—pointing to a potential organizational or leadership blind spot. Either way, it's feedback to get curious about and possibly respond to.

Don't make the mistake of dismissing it all as unproductive complaining (though some of it might be). Underneath most complaints are hidden values, commitments, or needs that aren't being met or even expressed. For example, in a discovery process with one company, a lot of people expressed concern about people getting burnt out. As we continued to dig into the data, we found out that what people really cared about was long-term sustainability and work/life balance. This insight then informed one of the company's core values.

Shadow Themes as a Polarity to Attend To

Another founding team we worked with had a clear theme emerge around "doing whatever it took" or "grit." In the focus groups, we heard a lot about a shadow theme of "burnout, no personal life, not friendly to employees with families." This is a classic polarity where two equally important values are out of balance. In this case, the value of "doing whatever it takes" was in a dynamic tension with work/life balance. The feedback was telling them that they might be over-indexed on one side of the polarity and need to adjust it going forward.

You can manage these polarities by explicitly including them in your Culture Code within a single theme. For instance, Netflix combined "Autonomy and Responsibility" as one of their core values. Autonomy works when combined with an equal amount of personal responsibility. Freedom without responsibility multiplied by hundreds of people can lead to a lot of chaos. Alternatively, you can have two different values that balance each other out. At The Motley Fool, the values of "Competitive—Play Fair, Play Hard, Play to Win" is balanced with the value of "Collaborative—Do Great Things Together."

DISTILLING YOUR CORE THEMES

Review the full picture across all of your themes. Walk through each theme and discuss as a group: Is including this theme in our Culture Code essential?

You're not looking for "nice-to-haves" or themes that make you say, "Yeah, that's sort of us." You're identifying the beliefs and behaviors that truly represent your company's unique identity, the beliefs that are indispensable aspects of your organization.

It's easiest to start by identifying the themes that inspire an emphatic "yes!" from the whole team and setting those aside. From there, edit and remix the remainder until you've arrived at core themes or values to proceed with.

We suggest aiming for 3–6 themes here, although it's hard to be prescriptive about this. Too many and your values are hard to remember. Too few and you'll leave out important aspects of who you are.

One word of caution here: as you distill your themes, there's often a desire to start finding the right words. Of course you'll want to capture any new phrasing or key words that surface during your conversations, but don't get lost in wordsmithing. Your initial focus should be identifying the essential themes. Finding the right words comes next.

One team we worked with had a theme titled "Sense of Togetherness." This theme had, by far, the most quotes and stories grouped beneath it. During focus groups that we conducted, most everyone shared this as something unique about their company. But when it came time to identify their core themes, no one felt it was a core part of who they were. Rather, one of the founders mentioned that the sense of togetherness seemed to be a byproduct of how committed everyone was to the other values that had been identified. For the moment, they removed the "Sense of Togetherness" bucket from their working list, and as they continued to refine their list, nothing seemed to be missing by excluding that idea. This is exactly how to work through the process of identifying your core values: continue to refine and distill until you've uniquely captured the true essence of who you are and what makes you your very best.

It's normal, even expected, that during this step your themes evolve significantly. One team that we worked with had a theme headlined "Responsible/Accountable for the Outcome." As we discussed it, we felt stuck. During the ongoing conversation, people kept mentioning that the theme was really about being responsible and accountable to the team. So we asked the question, "What's so important about the team?" The answer came quickly: "This is a team sport." As soon as it was said, you could feel the energy in the room rise. That phrase was the perfect articulation of what they valued: everyone doing their individual part, but all in the name of the team succeeding.

Pay Attention to What's Not Said

One other approach that many teams benefit from is looking at what *isn't being said* across your set of the theme buckets. Often a key concept jumps out as missing and sparks a new insight.

While guiding Castlight Health's leadership team through their Discovery and Design steps, after all the data was bucketed into themes and consolidated, what stood out most was what was missing: there was no mention of the customer. Their focus on the customer was so at the forefront of their work that people took it as a given. Noticing that this was missing was an "aha" moment that led to "Start with the Customer" being the first item in their Culture Code.

WHAT DO YOU DO IF YOU HAVE TOO MANY THEME BUCKETS?

Perfection (in design) is achieved not when there is nothing more to add, but rather when there is nothing more to take away.

—Antoine de Saint-Exupéry

At this point of the process, you may still have many theme buckets that you've identified. If so, then part of your task is to combine and distill your list into something more manageable. Most teams end up with between three and six buckets, which is the right amount. You don't want to leave out anything crucial. But you need your Culture Code to be short enough that everyone can actually remember it.

A helpful framework for creating a cohesive list of values (or anything for that matter) is MECE. Originally created at McKinsey in the late sixties, MECE stands for "mutually exclusive (ME) and collectively exhaustive (CE)."

When a list of values or categories is mutually exclusive, each item is distinct from other items. In other words, there is no overlap. For instance, if your list included "Collaborative" and "Good partners," you might consider combining these two into a single theme, as there is significant overlap between the two.

Your list of values also needs to be collectively exhaustive such that when you consider the entire set as a whole, it feels complete and is not missing anything. Getting to a mutually exclusive, collectively exhaustive list will go a long way in increasing the credibility of your list of values.

FINDING THE RIGHT WORDS

Once you've locked down your high-level themes, it's time to bring them fully to life as your core values. You can do this asynchronously in small work teams, or the entire team can work collectively in the same room. For each theme, as well as the entire Culture Code, discuss:

What best captures and communicates this value? Is it a single word? A phrase? A full descriptive sentence? Or is there an image, metaphor, or story that best articulates this value?

Follow the energy in the room during this step. Begin with the theme that has the most excitement and/or clarity around it.

Whenever you feel that you've hit an impasse, take a stretch break, and then pick up with a different value afterwards. It can also be helpful to sleep on things or even step back for a few days (sometimes even longer) to let ideas simmer.

Twilio, a cloud communication startup, has a value named "Draw the Owl." This value originated from an internet meme years ago that became widespread within the company. The meme was simply a two-step process for drawing an owl. Step 1 was "Draw some circles." Step 2 was "Draw the rest of the fucking owl."

How to draw an owl

1.   2.

1. Draw some circles   2. Draw the rest of the fucking owl

For Twilio, "Draw the Owl" is their way of capturing a theme of taking charge and figuring things out for yourself. They could just as easily have drafted the value as "Take Initiative," but "Draw the Owl" has so much more history, story, and energy. It's Twilio's own unique way of saying that taking initiative is a core part of who they are.

When Cricket Health was finalizing its first Culture Code, there was a theme around being bold, being courageous. And while there was widespread alignment around this as one of the final themes, no one was energized about it. It wasn't until one of the subgroups came back with "We Dare Mighty Things..." (an excerpt from a quote attributed to a speech by President Theodore Roosevelt) that the group felt excited about it.

INSPIRATION, NOT IMITATION OR COMPARISON

When we were designing the Culture Code at one of the businesses that I founded, I remember how fearful I was that our team might not be excited about our values. I spent hours online looking at other companies' values and mission statements. At first, this served as good inspiration. I noticed things that I liked and didn't like. It gave me new ideas about how our Culture Code might look and feel. But I quickly reached a point of diminishing returns when I began wishing our values were more like company X or Y's values. What I needed instead was to trust that we were creating something that was true for our company.

For your own inspiration, you'll find a handful of Culture Code examples at the end of this chapter, including thoughts on what makes them great. Use these examples to spark ideas on how to articulate your Culture Code, but resist any desire to compare or copy. You and your company are worthy of something uniquely your own. The creative effort to get there is worth it.

EVALUATING YOUR CULTURE CODE

After helping many companies create their own Culture Code and reviewing hundreds of other companies' Culture Codes, we've seen firsthand that all Culture Codes are not created equal. Some resonate and are fully embraced by everyone. Others fall flat.

The best Culture Codes consistently demonstrate four important qualities: authenticity, energy, brevity, and clarity. Once you've written the first draft of your Culture Code, evaluate it for these qualities.

1. Does it feel authentic?

Culture Codes aren't aspirational statements about who we think we need to be in the future. They are an articulation of who we already are when we are at our best. When you can look at the Culture Code and say, "Yeah, that's us," you'll know it's authentic to the company or team.

Part of that authenticity comes from the specific values and behaviors that get emphasized, and part of it comes from the language used to express the values. You need to get past people's healthy skepticism and BS meters, so make sure you've articulated your values in a way that resonates. Also, a Culture Code that acknowledges some of the shadow elements is more likely to feel authentic than one that just focuses on the positive.

2. Does it energize?

When we work with teams to help them clarify their values, if they aren't energized and inspired by the final product, then we either haven't found the right values or haven't found the right way to articulate those values.

For a Culture Code to work, it needs to feel compelling and motivating to the team. If it isn't energizing for you, it has no chance of resonating throughout the entire company.

3. Is it succinct?

Don't throw a laundry list at your team. That's too much to internalize. Aim for 3–6 concise, powerful values that are both easily understood and easily remembered.

4. Does it provide clarity?

An effective Culture Code provides clear guidance on how to make decisions and treat one another. It helps the team manage inevitable trade-offs, know what's important, and clearly state how they want to behave with each other. Your Culture Code should be self-explanatory enough that whether or not it's being embraced will be obvious and observable.

NAMING YOUR CULTURE CODE

Once you've arrived at a working version of your Culture Code, give it a name to make it easy to refer to.

Here are just a handful of options that we've seen used:

- Our DNA
- Our Values / Our Core Values
- Our Core Principles / Our First Principles
- The Hootsuite Manifesto
- Our Culture Code / The HubSpot Culture Code
- The Davita Way
- The Buffer Culture: Powered by Happiness
- Our 5 Commitments

- The Little Book of IDEO[4]
- Company Culture at
- How GitHub Works / How Google Works

The naming is important as it needs to be consistent with the look and feel of your company's culture. Choose the name that feels most aligned with what you've designed.

THREE EFFECTIVE CULTURE CODES
AND WHAT MAKES THEM GREAT

Here are some of our favorite Culture Codes that meet each of the four must-haves, plus some additional thoughts on what we think works really well about them.

Example 1: Cricket Health

First, we love that they lead off their Culture Code by taking a stand for their purpose and the kind of healthcare world they want to create.

---

4   Brown, Tim. "The Little Book of IDEO: Values." SlideShare, December 18, 2013. https://www.slideshare.net/timbrown/ideo-values-slideshare1?ref=.

Specifically, by stating that "Everyone is worthy," they are broadcasting their commitment to reinforce the dignity of all the people that will be touched by their products and services, including all potential employees (doctors, nurses, and other clinicians) as well as their current and future patients. Publicly stating this is an efficient way to attract the kind of people who also care about that mission.

Second, each statement has clear guidance on the desired mindset and observable behavior for each value. This will pay off later (and in fact already has) as they build out rituals and trainings to reinforce each value.

Example 2: Atlassian

Our values

They guide what we do, why we create, and who we hire.

Open company, no bullshit

Openness is root level for us. Information is open internally by default and sharing is a first principle. And we understand that speaking your mind requires equal parts brains (what to say), thoughtfulness (when to say it), and caring (how it's said).

Build with heart and balance

"Measure twice, cut once." Whether you're building a birdhouse or a business, this is good advice. Passion and urgency infuse everything we do, alongside the wisdom to consider options fully and with care. Then we make the cut, and we get to work.

Don't #@!% the customer

Customers are our lifeblood. Without happy customers, we're doomed. So considering the customer perspective - collectively, not just a handful - comes first.

Play, as a team

We spend a huge amount of our time at work. So the more that time doesn't feel like "work," the better. We can be serious, without taking ourselves too seriously. We strive to put what's right for the team first – whether in a meeting room or on a football pitch.

Be the change you seek

All Atlassians should have the courage and resourcefulness to spark change - to make better our products, our people, our place. Continuous improvement is a shared responsibility. Action is an independent one.

Atlassian's original Culture Code uses everyday conversational language, making the values easier to connect with and more energizing. Each value is coupled with a paragraph of description to create clarity, plus a custom-designed icon. The end result is a documented Culture Code that is authentic and evokes curiosity. You can't help but want to read the entire thing once you see it.

Example 3: Iterable

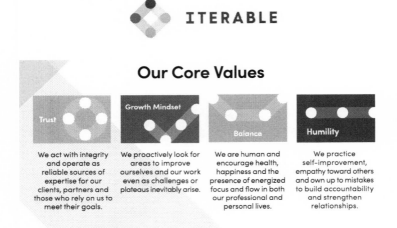

We love that Iterable kept it simple: four values. Everyone can remember what they are. We love how they have created a branded way of displaying their values by changing the order and shape that their logo dots make.

Iterable was founded in 2013. For the first two years, the company was finding its footing as a startup business. They elected to revisit their vision and values once they had expanded and established a more defined company personality. They grew from ten to twenty-five to fifty and were expecting to double again over the next eighteen months. Once they scaled, key members of the team got together to brainstorm an initial set of guiding values. They asked themselves, "What are some salient characteristics of our current people?" and two qualities were immediately obvious: humility and a growth mindset. As Andrew Boni tells it, "We had a lot of low ego people; people who wouldn't get offended easily (which became Humility)."

The other two values were more aspirational at the time. For instance, Trust—while not unique, was and is super central to Iterable's success. Customers needed to be able to trust the company with their data. Team members needed to be able to trust each other.

After fleshing out these values, Iterable rolled out the Culture Code at a whole-company offsite. Again, according to Andrew, what made the values stick was constant repetition and living these values at all times, through every interaction—internally, and with customers and partners. Their Culture Code appeared as the second slide of every presentation, at every all-hands meeting, and in every internal strategy deck.

This example is instructive because while Iterable didn't go through the whole process we outlined above, they were able to create a "meaningful and powerful" version of their Culture Code. This Culture Code guides their business decisions daily and has had a direct and positive impact on their growth to over seven hundred people and a $3 billion-plus valuation.

HOW TO KNOW WHEN YOU'RE DONE DESIGNING

While working recently with an early-stage startup on their first-ever Culture Code, we used the same process and evaluation criteria (authentic, energizing, succinct, and clear). At the end of a full-day meeting—after much wordsmithing and lively conversations—we went around the table and asked the question, "How do you feel when you look at this Culture Code?"

Here's a sample of what was shared:

"I came in skeptical, but now I'm a believer. This is way beyond my expectations."

"I am excited. This is authentic. I am impressed with how we came up with this."

"This is incredibly special and articulated with a lot of heart and soul."

"I feel validated in my decision to work here."

"I am at a loss for words. I am overwhelmed in a really good way."

"There is so much that is meaningful here."

Not only were the team members inspired, but so were we! It's a powerful experience when a group comes together to intentionally create a Culture Code that brings out the best version of themselves in their work and their life.

YOUR VALUES ARE JUST ONE PART OF YOUR CULTURE CODE

Congratulations on completing a central part of your Culture Code. If you want to make scaling culture easier, this will be just one of many culture-reinforcing artifacts that will emerge over time.

For example, in 2015, Slack—which had fewer than two hundred people at the time—created their first Culture Code at an offsite and then socialized the values with their directors. Over time, their culture evolved and so did their way of articulating it. In early 2016, I remember walking into the Slack office in San Francisco and seeing posters on the wall with sayings like, "Pretend that you're human" and "Nobody freak out." These cultural maxims conveyed simple but important reminders that influenced their work. Two years later, they refined their cultural articulation further by creating "the Four Attributes" (Smart, Humble, Hardworking, and Collaborative) that made hiring well and managing performance throughout the company easier.

Once you've captured the essence of who you are through the Design step, you'll feel a similar sense of clarity and truth to how you articulate your culture. And if you don't yet, then keep at it until you have something that's authentic, energizing, succinct, and clear. Once you can check off all four, call it good enough for now. Consider it a beta version of your Culture Code because, as you'll see shortly, you're going to have a chance to stress test it and further refine it in the next step.

After designing your Culture Code, you will have a powerful, foundational source of truth for your organization. The truth of who you are and what you value is no longer left to each individual to figure out. Suddenly, talking about this and giving feedback on this becomes possible, which brings you to the next step: Prototype.

CHECKLIST FOR THE DESIGN STEP

The Design step is about drafting a Culture Code that articulates your company's essence.

During the Design step you will:

- ☐ Consolidate and distill into themes all of the information gathered in the Discover step.
- ☐ Determine which themes are the must-haves of your Culture Code.
- ☐ Draft a Culture Code that uses the right words and imagery to best capture your essence.
- ☐ Verify that your Culture Code is (1) authentically yours, (2) powerfully energizing, (3) succinct, and (4) clarifying.
- ☐ Choose a name for your articulated set of values since "Culture Code" doesn't always feel right for everyone.

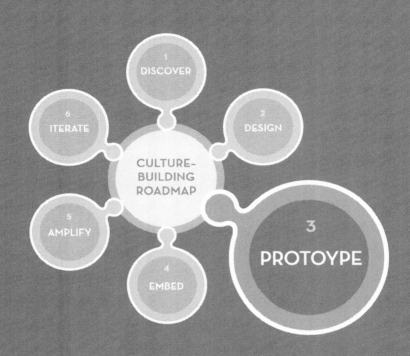

PROTOTYPE

Before you talk about your new
culture, walk around in it for a while.

We often get calls from leaders eager to codify their values because they recently read a book or heard someone talk about the importance of culture in creating a high-performing company. They'll ask for a day of facilitation with their senior team so that they can decide on values and share them with the rest of the company at their next all-hands meeting. The whole exercise feels like an effort to simply "check the box" and move on.

We were in the audience of one such all-hands meeting. Hundreds of employees sat in a big ballroom listening to a well-intentioned CEO walk through a slide deck of their values. When they got to the word *Integrity*, someone nearby snickered and said, "I wonder if these values apply to them as well?"

These cynical, eye-rolling moments happen all the time. Most companies, once they've designed some form of Culture Code, are in a hurry to hand it off to their teams. The Culture Code gets rushed out the door in a mix of excitement, anxiety, and a desire to get back to work. While well-intentioned, this is little more than wishful culture-building and introduces needless risk to the organization.

If your initial articulation of your Culture Code isn't fully dialed in, there's a possibility that the rushed rollout will be seen in some ways as misguided, untrue, or even bullshit. Even worse, like that CEO in the ballroom, if your leadership isn't perceived as being aligned with the values and behaviors stated in your Culture Code, you will lose credibility.

Instead of rushing the process, we're going to first prototype your Culture Code within your leadership team by (1) activating your Culture Code as a daily practice and (2) creating a regular feedback loop about where you are living your values and where you are not living your values. Think of this as a beta test: a chance to learn what works and doesn't work in a low-risk environment.

Prototyping refines your Culture Code before any attempts at making a big splash or trying to scale its impact. Plus, through prototyping, you start cultivating your culture within your leadership team so that it's concentrated enough to begin affecting the rest of the organization.

HOW TO PROTOTYPE AND TEST YOUR CULTURE CODE

Culture drives behavior and behavior drives culture.

Now that you have a Culture Code as an expression of your company's essence, you are ready to start translating those good intentions and words into action. Since the most visible expression of culture is behavior, this is the place to start.

Start by identifying key observable behaviors that, when demonstrated, bring your Culture Code to life; then adopt those behaviors through explicit agreements. This step is to be led by the founders and core leadership team, not your people or HR function. The leaders' behaviors must align with and be tested against your Culture Code.

To do this, set aside a couple of hours in the next week or two for your leadership team to walk through the following steps to launch your culture prototype.

Step 1: Identify Behaviors Aligned with Your Culture Code

As a group, walk through your Culture Code and, for each of the articulated values, discuss:

1. What observable behaviors would bring this value to life?
2. What behaviors are clearly not an expression of the value?

In exploring these, you're looking to hone in on specific behaviors that, if practiced consistently, would build the culture that you intend.

For example, if your Culture Code has a stated value of "Empathy for Others," you might list behaviors like:

71

- Listening before speaking
- Beginning every meeting with a personal check-in from each person
- Being curious about other people's perspectives
- Every week, talking to one of your business's customers

You'll likely come up with some behaviors that are both specific (e.g., "Beginning every meeting with a personal check-in") and others that are more conceptual (e.g., "Listening before speaking").

Capture any and all ideas from the brainstorm on a whiteboard. Encourage people to riff off one another, but don't spend time evaluating ideas just yet. Using Post-it notes and grouping similar ideas together can be a helpful method for surfacing ideas in a timely manner. This is especially useful for focusing the conversation into sets of themes in larger groups.

About five minutes per value is usually plenty of time to create a short, meaningful list.

Step 2: Commit to Practicing High-Leverage Cultural Behaviors

Next, take your list of value-aligned behaviors and identify 2–4 that have the most leverage for your prototype. High-leverage behaviors are those that you stand to learn the most from during your prototyping step. These are never the most natural or easy ones. The behaviors that you'll learn from are the ones that feel edgy, maybe even risky.

Two questions can help you spot high-leverage behaviors:

- Which behaviors have the highest potential to positively impact our culture?
- Which behaviors feel especially challenging for us to put into practice?

As a team, decide on a select few behaviors that (1) will help you learn and (2) you're all willing to commit to.

A couple of years ago, we facilitated an offsite for the executive team of a thirty-person company. They were committed to building their culture, but as they were in the midst of raising their Series B round of funding, they didn't feel they had the bandwidth for a big overhaul. They decided to establish a simple yet focused set of three agreements for how they would interact with each other.

Those three agreements were:

* **Be curious, debate, and commit:** We commit to staying curious even if we think we are right. We leave the room aligned.
* **Be coachable:** We ask for, and are receptive to, feedback.
* **Communicate without blame:** We commit to speaking directly to the person with whom we have an issue or concern. No gossip.

And then, throughout the course of their fundraising, they practiced.

Now that "Be curious, debate, and commit" was one of the team's cultural aspirations, they began noticing moments when curiosity didn't seem present in a conversation. Anytime this happened in a meeting or conversation, it was acknowledged. And because they were naming it, a new "culture-building choice" became available. The group would choose to intentionally shift their mindset from one of "listening to be right" to one of "listening to learn."

These aren't intended to be "gotcha" moments where someone is blamed or shamed for acting a certain way. Rather, these are learning moments where you gain deeper clarity on both the phrasing of your values and how you might fully embody them in building your culture.

The result of the team's prototyping was that, post-fundraise, they already had a strong start in building the culture that they wanted to create. The existing team had noticed the shift and it was clearer that scaling the company would mean only hiring curious people from now on. It was a powerful outcome from a small group with high-leverage commitments.

Step 3: Learn from the "Not Culture" Moments without Flinching

When behaviors misaligned with company culture occur, most people sweep them under the rug. But if you want to build an intentional culture, you need to start acknowledging them. You're even going to want to deliberately seek them out as opportunities to better understand and reinforce the desired culture.

Make explicit agreements with your leadership team around how you'll give or receive feedback when these moments occur:

1. What will you say, and how will you say it?
2. How will you hold each other accountable?
3. How will you respond when someone offers you feedback?

Your responses to these questions frame how you'll maintain an ongoing dialogue during the prototyping process. Be explicit and ensure agreement before you move forward. We've seen teams answer the above questions in a variety of ways.

One team that exhibited high levels of trust with one another committed to give each other report cards every week at their executive team meeting. In doing so, they began building credibility by ritually demonstrating their serious efforts to embody the values and behaviors that they wanted to see more of at the company. It made them better at spotting potential hires who would be able to do the same. And they became a higher-functioning team, all by simply committing to practice and provide feedback to one another.

Another team we worked with decided that it would be easier for each person to hold themselves accountable first before offering feedback to each other. At every other regular leadership team meeting, they would spend 5–15 minutes highlighting culture-in-action moments as well as missed opportunities. Each person would report on at least one personal example of them demonstrating a specific culture practice and one example of where they had room for improvement. They used these two sentence stems:

- "I reinforced the (insert specific culture value/behavior here) when I (insert specific moment here)."
- "I missed an opportunity to reinforce (insert specific culture value/behavior here) when I (insert specific moment here)."

Be specific and personal in naming behaviors. If you have a value of "Always Being Open to New Ideas," then statements like "I need to work on being more open to new ideas" are meaningless to make and will probably change nothing. It would be more instructive and useful to say, "I missed an opportunity to reinforce *the value of being open to new ideas* when *Sarah gave me feedback at our product review meeting and I got defensive.*" Being specific conveys to the rest of your team that you are paying attention to your own behavior and are actively engaged in being consistent with your espoused Culture Code.

Some teams we've worked with have even come up with their own code words or prompts to make in-the-moment feedback easier. A CEO who had a habit of stating their views as gospel truth asked their team to respond with "You seem decided on this; are you open to other views?" This simple, agreed-upon feedback tool helped open conversations back toward their stated value around curiosity.

Step 4: Schedule Your Next Prototyping Check-In

Wrap up your prototype kickoff session by scheduling the next meeting for your leadership team to assess your prototype together. For most teams, we suggest regrouping in 2–4 weeks' time.

What's most important is that you're actually prototyping: practicing the behaviors in the day-to-day and having ongoing conversations about them. When you reconvene, use the following guide to assess the outcome of your prototyping process.

HOW TO ASSESS YOUR PROTOTYPE

After testing out your Culture Code during the Prototype step, you'll encounter one of three outcomes—each is, in its own way, a successful prototyping process.

Outcome #1: Something in your Culture Code doesn't feel quite right. This could be anything from discomfort with certain wording to a realization that part of the code doesn't hold true for your team. One way or another, your prototype has shown you that your Culture Code needs further revision. If this happens, simply loop back to the Design step to make the necessary changes before once again prototyping your Culture Code. Don't be discouraged. Making revisions is often quick, and your culture will benefit for years to come.

Outcome #2: There's consensus that your Culture Code feels right, yet the leadership team is struggling to fully live it. Maybe it's been surprisingly busy at work in recent weeks. Perhaps you've not entirely followed through on giving one another feedback. Whatever the reason, it is powerful for teams to be honest with themselves about reaching this outcome. You should simply continue to prototype further. As a team, consider modifying the values and behaviors you've been prototyping, or consider different ways of providing one another with feedback. Most importantly, stay focused on learning.

Outcome #3: There's consensus that your Culture Code feels right, and the leadership team is doing a good job of living the values.

Feedback is given regularly and acted upon when received. There's a feeling of momentum and clarity on how the Culture Code can be brought to life even more fully inside the organization. The Culture Code continues to feel authentic and energizing. Most importantly, it feels alive. This is the beauty of the prototyping process because when you're ready to proceed, you can feel it. There's a sense that what you've created is not only authentic but also will help you stay true to what's important over time.

EMBED YOUR CULTURE CODE BEFORE GOING PUBLIC

Once you have confidence in your leadership team's ability to demonstrate the culture in action, it's almost time to share it with the rest of the company. But before you do, we recommend that you read through the Embed chapter to start to ground the Culture Code into the artifacts, processes, and daily rituals that guide how you work. Then, in the Amplify chapter, we'll offer a guide for your public launch.

We have seen companies rush into a splashy culture launch event before doing some of the work to bring their culture to life, and this can have the opposite effect of what you want. You want to build enough physical evidence for the culture to make it easy for people to believe in and buy into. By doing this work in advance, you will help your launch event gain a lot more momentum because you will have more evidence and support available for scaling culture.

After completing your prototype, you can think of your Culture Code as a validated blueprint for building the vibrant, effective culture that you want to have. But the blueprint isn't the building. That comes next as we turn toward embedding your Culture Code — bringing to life your most important values in the day-to-day work that you do.

CHECKLIST FOR THE PROTOTYPE STEP

This step is about putting your newly drafted Culture Code to the test before you consider rolling it out to the entire company.

During the Prototype step:
- ☐ Identify a list of aligned and misaligned behaviors for each of your stated values.
- ☐ Commit to practicing a select few behaviors that have the most leverage for your culture—the behaviors that, if you truly embrace them, will transform the trajectory of the business, the team, and yourself.
- ☐ Establish accountability for practicing these behaviors along with agreed-upon methods for giving one another feedback.
- ☐ Schedule a time to reconvene to discuss the outcome of your prototype.

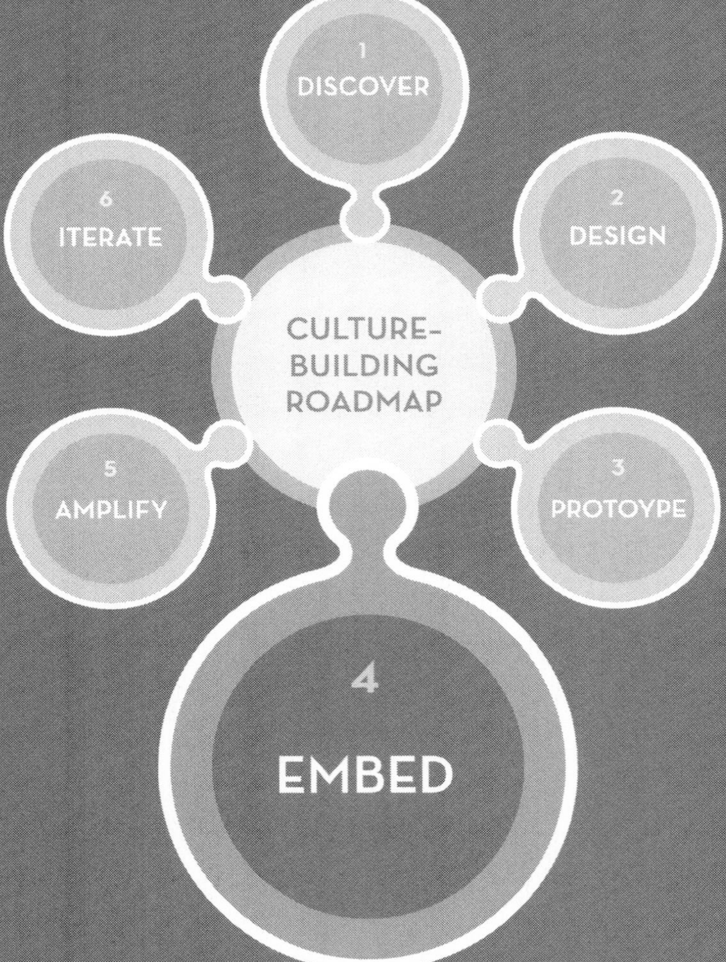

CULTURE-BUILDING ROADMAP

1 DISCOVER

2 DESIGN

3 PROTOYPE

4 EMBED

5 AMPLIFY

6 ITERATE

STEP 4

EMBED

From Culture Code to
Culture in Action

With your validated Culture Code in hand, you have a blueprint for creating cultural leverage in your business. Here the real work begins as you activate that Culture Code by embedding it into the daily functioning of your company.

Most companies never reach this step in their culture-building. They get excited and are in a hurry after their Culture Code is created. They'll hold a company all-hands meeting (a good idea, just not the time for it yet) and they'll make posters. Seriously. They'll print out their fresh, new values, announce them to the company by sticking them on the wall, and then hope that things magically change. But words on a wall don't mean much of anything unless they're lived out.

What the teams that do this miss is that by stopping culture efforts here, they introduce a new risk to their business that they wouldn't have if they'd never defined and announced their values in the first place. It's the *risk of the revolving door of talent*, and it goes something like this:

With your values in hand, a savvy recruiter can spin your culture to sound great to a candidate. And so you'll meet more and better candidates. During interviews, you can expect candidates to ask some form of the question, "What is the culture like here?" Your values make it easy to offer a great-sounding answer. You'll see the interviewees' eyes light up as you share bold statements about what's important to you. You might even be able to point to the posters on the wall. And they'll think, *This seems like a different place, a place I want to be a part of.* More and better people will join your team. But on their first day, they'll notice things are different than they expected. They'll assume it's an exception. Day two...more of the same. Confusion, skepticism, and disappointment will follow. Most won't stay long. Over time, your Glassdoor ratings will start to reflect this, and soon you'll be right back in the next interview giving the same answer to "What is the culture like here?" as you try to convince the next person to join. If the values aren't alive, the door will continue to revolve. Exceptional people will join; exceptional people will leave.

Articulating your values can attract talent. Living your values, by embedding them in the day-to-day, is what makes new hires want to stay.

EMBEDDING CULTURE IN THREE DIMENSIONS

The teams that are best at bringing their values to life are systematic in reinforcing culture across three dimensions of their business that we call the I/WE/IT—an adaptation of Integral Theory's Four Quadrants Framework.[5]

- I: The individual, personal. (How each of us behaves and leads. Your personal values and your relationship with your company values.)
- WE: Collective, interpersonal. (How you relate to others, how you communicate with each other, how you hold meetings.)
- IT: Organizational, impersonal. (The processes, structures and systems that most impact the business and the people in it. Your hiring, onboarding, and performance management processes. Your brand's look, feel, and story. Your office space. How you make decisions.)

Focusing on each of these three dimensions powerfully influences organizational health and business success. In fact, we've witnessed how underdevelopment on any of the three dimensions limits your company's ability to grow and thrive.

---

5 Wilber, Ken. "What Are the Four Quadrants?" Integral Life, October 28, 2014. https://integrallife.com/four-quadrants/.

THREE DIMENSIONS OF COMPANY CULTURE

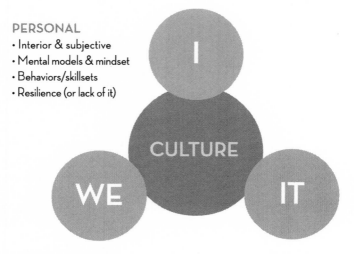

PERSONAL
- Interior & subjective
- Mental models & mindset
- Behaviors/skillsets
- Resilience (or lack of it)

INTERPERSONAL
- Relationships
- Rapport & communication
- Culture, group norms & rituals
- Collaboration & teamwork

IMPERSONAL
- External & objective
- Systems & structures
- Procedures & processes
- Goals & metrics

For the rest of this chapter, we will share with you our embedding culture model, with the top strategies and focus areas we recommend in each of the three dimensions. We'll begin with the interpersonal glue (the WE dimension) that connects people together, then we'll share a variety of ways to embed your culture in day-to-day processes and work (the IT dimension), and finally we'll conclude with the importance of each individual's behaviors (the I dimension) in shaping your culture.

A COMPANY'S CULTURE IS REINFORCED
THROUGH A VARIETY OF ACTIVITIES

PLACES TO EMBED CULTURE

Team and Company Rituals That Create Connection

Creating rituals around when and how people gather continues to be one of the highest-leverage methods we've seen for building culture.

A ritual is simply "a sequence of activities involving gestures, words, and objects, performed in a sequestered place and according to a set sequence." A handshake or fist bump when you meet someone is an example of a ritual. So is singing "Take Me Out to the Ball Game" during the seventh-inning stretch at a baseball game.

Rituals create shared experiences, build relationships, and add deeper meaning amongst groups of people.

You might already have some rituals at your company. And you will certainly want to consider how you might create new rituals to become part of the fabric of your lived culture.

Anytime two or more people are gathered is an opportunity for a connective ritual:

- Team and project meetings
- Offsites
- Office parties
- All-company/All-hands meetings
- Board meetings

Rituals can serve many different purposes:

- To welcome new people (these might be rituals embedded into your onboarding process)
- To celebrate wins
- To acknowledge failures and learnings
- To reinforce a specific value
- To say goodbye to people who are moving on

Consider:

- What are the rituals that already exist on your team that you want to encourage more of?
- Where could you add new rituals to reinforce your company values and create moments of connection?

Aim to create and encourage rituals that are actionable and that solve real problems. Treat them like an experiment. Commit to trying them out for a specific period of time, and then collect some data on how they went and decide if you want to keep them, improve them, or let them go. Some rituals that make sense when you are small and scrappy will not work when you are three hundred people.

One team we worked with had named "Building a Business Is a Team Sport" as one of their core values. They brought this to life by taking turns facilitating team meetings. This created new experimentation with agendas and approaches, which led to their team meetings truly becoming more of a team sport.

Another company's value, "Here to Help Our Customers," was ritualized by having every employee (including the executives) spend at least one day a year answering customer support requests.

"We Care about Each Individual Person" was made a part of one team's onboarding by having every new employee create a short five- to eight-slide deck introducing themselves to the company. Then all decks were cataloged on a wiki to make it easy to get to know everyone.

One team's "We Are a Work in Progress" value inspired the ritual of a weekly internal demo day for anyone to showcase what they were working on. Often the less complete something was, the more applause the person received for being willing to show off their unpolished work in progress.

Another team's "Relationships Matter" value meant that every meeting began with a personal check-in that invited each person to share "what it's like to be you right now." Even if 25 percent of the meeting time was spent doing the check-in, the time felt well used. Relationships were built and everyone was reminded why their company was such a special place to be a part of.

One team's "We Are Open and Honest with One Another" value led to a ritual of holding quarterly founder AMAs (Ask Me Anything) that were forums for surfacing any and all questions within the organization. They also would cc the entire company on monthly investor update emails. Plus, all key metrics were shared openly within the company. Each was a small choice with a meaningful impact in creating a more open and honest workplace. And there was evidence that this worked. Junior engineers would approach the founders in the kitchen with probing questions about the product or organizational strategy. This open inquiry created a better flow of information and often informed a better approach. This type of result is evidence that your values are accelerating the business, an indicator that you're finding effective means for embedding your culture in the work.

Take the rituals already happening in your organization and dial them up to be more noticeable, more impactful. And experiment with new rituals that align with your values. Some will stick and transform the impact of your work.

Increase the Quality of Your Conversations

The Quality of the Conversation = The Quality of the Culture

When we do culture assessments for new companies, we start by observing a few different groups holding their regular meetings. And, even though people know that we're observing them and they are trying to be on their best behavior, we usually witness a pattern of mediocre conversations or, worse, "death by bullet points" with little or no clarifying conversations.

Most commonly, one or two people will dominate the conversation while others disengage. In one meeting, we even observed a person texting beneath the table about how poorly the meeting was going.

During these mediocre conversations, positions and decisions are abundantly advocated for, yet there is a surprising lack of inquiry occurring. Interruptions, side conversations, and a lack of full engagement dominate the room. Unfortunately, this has become the standard for many group conversations.

Low-quality conversation creates a dampening effect on everything you do. Specifically, it affects:

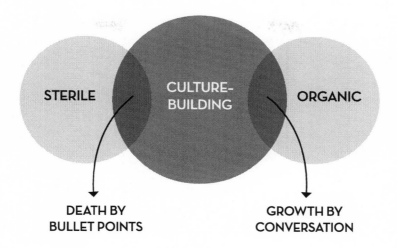

- What gets discussed, what doesn't get discussed
- Who gets to offer input and who doesn't
- How much energy is generated (or lost)
- The capacity of a team to tackle difficult subjects together
- How quickly a group can learn from current data and past actions

Upgrading the quality of your conversations is a direct path to improving the interpersonal dimension of your culture.

Good conversations have four crucial components:

1. **Informing:** How much are people revealing? Is all important information being put on the table? Is the information being shared in a kind, thoughtful way so that others are also encouraged to engage?

2. **Asking:** How curious (or not) are people? Do people ask open-ended questions that they don't already know the answer to?

3. **Listening**: How well do people bring their full presence and attention to the person speaking?
4. **Reflecting**: How well do people reflect what they are hearing in such a way that others feel heard and feel that their input is valued?

The best way to increase the quality of the conversations you are having is to train people in the skills above, which enable great conversations, and to follow these basic principles:

1. Have *one* conversation at a time. This means one person talking at a time as well as focusing on one topic at a time. It's an invitation for teams to slow down the conversational speed a bit, in order to become more efficient in the long run.
2. Balance inquiry and advocacy. Conversations that lack curiosity are breeding grounds for conflict and misalignment. To find common ground, disrupt the pattern with questions that inquire into the positions being advocated for.
3. GRRRF! (Get really real, really fast). Move quickly through the superficial stage of conversations (or drop it altogether) in favor of revealing and disclosing deeper thoughts, feelings, hopes, and fears. This is a shortcut to building a culture of increased psychological safety, candor, and warmth.
4. Lean forward, lean back. If you are someone who is quick to jump in and say what you think during conversations, can you "lean back" to create space for the introverts to "lean forward" and share their perspectives? And if you're one who is usually quieter, can you "lean forward" a bit more to share your experience? Looking through this lens, every conversation becomes a visible demonstration of the culture. By attending to the quality of the conversation we are having, we are directly attending to the quality of our team and company culture.

The ability to engage in high-quality conversations is a skillset that can be learned. Many of our clients have asked us to spend a couple hours at an offsite focusing on skill building to give everyone a common language and common approach. Others have created a basic skills workshop that they ask all their employees to take in the first year. However you tackle it, investing in your collective ability to have the conversations you need to have will pay for itself many times over.

Embedding Culture in Your Hiring

If you're currently growing your team, ensure you've embedded your culture in the hiring process. Doing so helps attract the right people, makes discerning who is a good fit easy, and increases your ability to attract the best talent. More than anything else, your hiring process needs to drive to a clear answer on the question: Does this person naturally live our values?

Buffer is one of our favorite examples of this. Their first stated value is "Default to Transparency," and even before you consider entering their hiring process, you get a full peek into the company and how they hire. You can calculate what your salary would be,[6] see others' salaries, and see how diverse the team is.[7] Even company revenue is public.[8] And all of this information is linked in the footer of the Buffer home page.

Not everyone appreciates this level of transparency, but those that do are certainly going to be intrigued by Buffer's approach. Their commitment to transparency also led them to publish a

---

6 Hubbard, Caryn, and Jenny Terry. "The Next Evolution of Transparent Salaries: Our New Remote-First Formula and Updated Salary Calculator." Buffer, December 6, 2017. https://buffer.com/resources/salary-formula/.

7 Seiter, Courtney. "Building a More Inclusive Startup: Introducing the Diversity Dashboard." Buffer, June 24, 2015. https://buffer.com/resources/diversity-dashboard/.

8 "Transparent Revenue." Buffer. Accessed May 11, 2022. https://buffer.com/revenue.

glimpse into their entire hiring process,[9] so if you do choose to apply, you'll have an idea of what to expect.

We help many of our clients identify a small set of (usually around three) primary qualities or behaviors that they want to prioritize in interviews. Then we develop targeted interview questions to elicit insightful responses.

Here are some example interview questions focused on the value of "compassion":

- "Give me an example of a time you received or had to deliver direct *and* compassionate feedback."
- "Would you share an example of when you were able to step into someone else's shoes to better see their point of view? What changed for you by doing so?"
- "Tell me about a time when you cared or had a deep sense of compassion for someone at work, and what you did."

Here are some example interview questions for the value of "mission-driven":

- "What do you know about our mission?"
- "In what ways does our mission align with your work and your life?"
- "What does it mean to you to work for a mission-driven company?"

For each question, we help the company develop a guide that includes a rubric of possible responses that helps them evaluate candidates. For instance:

---

9   Seiter, Courtney. "How We Hire: A Look Inside Our Hiring Process." Buffer, March 14, 2018. https://buffer.com/resources/hiring-process/.

Question: Tell me about a time when you successfully created buy-in and consensus on a group project.

Rubric: A strong answer to this question should include:

* Willingness to listen to others and be empathetic
* Evidence of structured thinking / problem solving (e.g., "My plan to create buy-in was to do x, y, and z.")
* Strong communication skills (e.g., the candidate explained the answer to the question clearly)

A hiring guide that captures these types of focused questions and an easy-to-use rubric can go a long way toward helping your team hire more great people. A well-defined rubric can also help combat conscious and unconscious bias in your hiring process.

Onboarding People into Your Culture

Once you've hired the right person, your onboarding is where they are introduced to your culture. Onboarding done well creates clarity and helps people contribute faster. A better onboarding program can decrease ramp time by 30 percent and can improve new hire retention by 82 percent and productivity by over 70 percent.[10]

Your onboarding experience should not only be a delightful welcome to the team but also reinforce the norms of how you work together. During onboarding, aim to create meaningful encounters with your culture, so much so that a new person can't help but feel a part of the team. There are all sorts of ways that your values can come to life here.

---

10 Laurano, Madeline. "The True Cost of a Bad Hire." BDO, August 2015. https://www.bdo.com/getattachment/fc989309-6824-4ad6-9f8d-9ef1138e3d42/the-true-cost-of-a-bad-hire.pdf.aspx?lang=en-US.

Many companies send new team members swag (T-shirts, stickers, socks, etc.) as a tangible symbol of their culture and a way to welcome new team members to the tribe. We've seen some founders who were so particular about getting this right that they worked through multiple revisions of both the swag and the box it came in before it was ever given out.

A new team member's first day, first week, and first months are also important parts of the onboarding experience.

At Twenty20, when someone accepted a job offer, their new team would record a short welcome video that would be turned into a GIF and sent to them via text. Even before their first day, they'd get something special and personal from their team.

At Davita, new team members spend half of their first day at a highly interactive and experiential workshop that introduces the company's culture and how they work together. They follow this up a few months later with an optional two-day Leadership Academy experience. Hundreds of new Davita employees gather for these events, which are a combination of an exploration of their values, a skills workshop, and a rally. Attendees leave feeling bought in on the company and deeply connected with the people and mission.

Slack provides a similar experiential introduction to their culture, but not until later in a team member's first week. Rather, on a new hire's first day at Slack, they head straight into doing actual work. This looks different for different roles. Developers at Slack will write and push code on their first day. Support team members will likely answer customer support tickets. It's a highly practical first day designed to have each new employee experience the Slack culture through doing work.

With any experiential cultural onboarding, include operators and key leaders as much as possible so the material stays grounded in the actual work versus becoming too much of a HR-led process. Motley Fool does this well, even as a larger organization. They use a welcome video led by their CEO to walk through how they work as well as highlighting key culture principles. Similarly, Castlight Health built in a three-hour values exploration that was taught by different executives. And the team at Nuna, a healthcare data and analytics startup, brought together both day-to-day operators and their HR leaders to offer a highly practical onboarding experience.

Performance Management

Most companies are slow to make performance management a priority, and when they do, performance management is defined too narrowly—as in "results are all that matter." This approach tends to lead to a system where "talented jerks"—those smart, dedicated people who get a lot done, and might even be considered "rockstar performers" but disempower and disenfranchise other people along the way—thrive. And while results certainly matter, you also want to measure people's performance against your values.

We suggest two things to kick this off:

1. Institute a feedback-friendly team culture from the very start.
2. Build out feedback loops that include feedback on both results *and* impact on others.

How to Create a Feedback-Friendly Team Culture: Pull > Push

It's a lot easier to create a feedback-friendly culture by setting an expectation that everyone requests feedback instead of trying to "push feedback" onto people. You can do this by teaching a basic feedback protocol and then having everyone regularly ask for feedback. There are dozens of codified approaches that you can adopt from Radical Candor, Crucial Conversations, Fierce Conversations, or the tried and true feedback model called SBI (Situation, Behavior, Impact). It doesn't matter which one you choose; just choose one, and do a workshop or a book club on the topic and start practicing.

For a short primer on SBI, check out the additional Resources section at www.scalewithoutlosingyoursoul.com.

Build Out Feedback Loops That Include Feedback on Both Results *and* Impact on Others

What you reward, talk about, and don't talk about in relation to people's performance reinforces what matters in your organization.

This starts with explicitly including culture and values in the way you define the expectations for specific roles.

Performance conversations should include both dimensions of performance: results and their impact on others. In other words, *what* did the person do or not do, achieve or not achieve (as measured by...), and *how* did the way they did it impact others around them?

Doing this up front will keep culture and impact on culture in every performance conversation. It will stimulate individual and team reflection on how you are (or are not) living the culture you aspire to.

HOW TO AVOID A CULTURE THAT TOLERATES "HIGH-PERFORMING JERKS"

One of our past clients, a Canadian Crown company that provides credit and financial services to farmers, hired one of us to help facilitate a leadership summit for their top leaders. Under the leadership of their CEO and head of human resources, they had invested heavily in redefining their values and defining ten high-performance behaviors (prototype!). They then offered high-quality experiential training in these behaviors for all of their top leaders.

But they had plateaued in their progress. A key obstacle they identified was that not all of the senior leaders were buying into the effort. They were tolerating too many "high-performing jerks" who drove business results but ignored these leadership behaviors. This happened because their leadership evaluation rubric only focused on results, with each person given a rating from 5 (highest) to 1 (lowest) on how well they met performance expectations. The scale looked something like this:

- 5: "Far exceeding expectations"
- 4: "Exceeding expectations"
- 3: "Meeting expectations"
- 2: "Partly meeting expectations"
- 1: "Not meeting expectations"

The problem with this system is that it didn't include any evaluation of how the leader impacted others. Individuals were regularly promoted to senior levels of the organization due to their stellar performance in booking revenue, even though their team's engagement and retention scores were the lowest in the company.

At this leadership summit, we ironed out a new performance evaluation rubric that included both results and culture. We used the same 1–5 rating above but also added a second column that included another 1–5 rating on cultural impact:

- 5: "Culture Champion" (role model for values and leadership behaviors)
- 4: "100 percent accountable" (accountability is one of their core behaviors; this is a person who is willing to demonstrate responsibility for both results

and their impact on others as evidenced by asking
for and being receptive and responsive to feedback
and being coachable)

- 3: "Making an effort" (not perfect but willing, as
  demonstrated by a willingness to work on their own
  blind spots and past leadership habits in an active
  way)
- 2: "Needs improvement"
- 1: "Not meeting expectations"

Once the company instituted this evaluation rubric, it forced
them to have the hard conversations about how to manage
someone who is "Far exceeding expectations" (5) on results
but "Needs improvement" (2) in terms of culture. With this
new system, a person with these ratings would no longer
be promotable. Furthermore, two consecutive reviews with
a "Needs improvement" rating (or lower) would result
in the leader being offered coaching and being put on a
performance improvement plan.

These changes led to some leaders moving on or being
let go in the short term, but the company also became a
better place to work. Within two years, they were named
one of the top ten places to work in Canada because culture
had become a part of how they measured performance.

Keeping Culture as a Strategic Priority

One of the biggest pitfalls in culture-building is that culture efforts
get treated as separate from the real work. When other objectives
and initiatives are seen as more important, culture takes a back
seat.

This is actually quite easy to fix: embed your culture into your strategy and your objectives and key results (OKRs). One of the simplest ways to do this is to focus one of your top OKRs on a specific measurable culture outcome.

Asana is one of our favorite examples of culture embedded in strategy. Their core value "Reject False Tradeoffs" is intentionally interwoven into their strategy in that they "reject the notion that strong business results and a thriving culture are mutually exclusive."[11] Culture is core to their strategy: not just a nice-to-have or an add-on, but a part of achieving the business results that they aim to.

Your Public Brand

You can also embed culture externally through how you engage your customers and infuse your public brand with key elements of your values.

Craig Wilson, the former marketing lead at Patagonia, makes a strong bottom-line business case for the importance of tying your values into your public brand, stating,

"The path to long-term, sustainable loyalty is based on an unspoken agreement: You believe what I believe and I believe what you believe. Now we can do business from a place of trust and inspiration."[12]

It's no surprise, then, that any interaction with Patagonia brings you into contact with their value of sustainability. Go to their website, open their catalog, or visit a store and you will see how much

---

11 Binder, Anna. "How We've Designed a Culture That Fuels Our Business Results." Asana, November 7, 2019. https://blog.asana.com/2019/11/culture-fuels-business-results/.

12 Wilson, Craig. The Compass and the Nail: How the Patagonia Model of Loyalty Can Save Your Business, and Might Just Save the Planet. Los Angeles, California: Rare Bird Books, 2015.

the planet matters to them. It is core to both their strategy and their brand.

Another example is Buffer, whose value of "Default to Transparency and Communicate with Clarity" has led them to openly share their entire product roadmap publicly.[13] If you're a customer, or considering becoming one, you know exactly what you're going to get today and in the future.

People trust and want to buy from brands like these that live their values in public. This is not only because we often share their values but also because we admire them for standing for something.

The Work Platforms and the Tools You Use

Your team interacts with a variety of work tools every day, making them high-frequency, and usually underutilized, touchpoints for culture-building. Both the tools that you use and how you use them matters. Getting intentional about how you set up, use, and even name your tools can be another way to embed your values.

Consider creating a guidance document that trains people how to optimize their use of the tools, and include this as part of their onboarding.

Slack, in particular, is a tool that we've seen used both well and poorly to build culture. Thoughtfully setting up channels, naming them clearly, and intentionally moving conversations into the right public channels are easy wins.

We helped set up Slack channels for each of one company's core values. Then, using the Slack Reacji Channeler,[14] an emoji was assigned to each of the culture values/channels so anyone—in one

---

13 Hitch, Jim. "Building in the Open: Introducing Buffer's Transparent Product Roadmap." Buffer, April 12, 2016. https://buffer.com/resources/transparent-product-roadmap/.

14 "Reacji Channeler." Built By Slack. Accessed May 11, 2022. https://reacji-channeler.builtbyslack.com/.

click—could send other Slack conversations to dedicated channels for each company value. With one click, people now could acknowledge culture moments in a public way that invited others to do the same. With these Slack channels, the team has a growing catalog and timeline of stories and moments where their values were lived out.

Org Structure and Management Systems

There is one last "IT dimension" focus area worth covering that many assume is fixed: your org structure and management systems. Many founders don't even know they have a choice about how they structure their companies. The vast majority of companies follow the same mainstream default playbook with a hierarchy of people, where certain roles (managers and senior managers) are imbued with decision-making and budget authority, while other roles have less or none.

Embedded in traditional organizational structures are two primary default settings: (1) they assign decision rights and budget authority to a people hierarchy, which typically provides more authority as you move up the ladder; and (2) that people hierarchy (org chart) becomes the de facto achievement ladder for almost everyone in the company. Most people who want to progress must now become people managers (whether or not they are so inclined) to achieve significant career advancement.

Over the last 20 years, new models and approaches have emerged for how you can structure your company. Companies like Blinkist, Zappos, Medium, Nucor Steel, Semco, Morning Star Tomatoes, Haier, and Patagonia have demonstrated new ways of organizing their work.[15]

---

15 "Cases for Inspiration." Reinventing Organizations Wiki. Accessed May 11, 2022. https://reinventingorganizationswiki.com/en/cases/.

We'll touch briefly on two of these structures: B Corporations and Holacracy. Please note that we offer these cutting-edge approaches not because we believe they are the right choice for everyone, but rather to open your mind to thinking about ways that you might organize to more fully express your purpose and your values beyond profit. These new approaches offer more transparency, less hierarchy, participatory governance and decision-making, self-management, increased complexity awareness, and a company structure organized around a purpose greater than profit.

B CORPORATIONS

B Corporations are businesses that are structured to pursue both profit and purpose and certified as such by B Lab, the B Corporation governing body. These types of businesses are designed to create transparency and accountability around the full impact of the company's activities. To be considered, your company must undertake a full impact assessment to evaluate how the business's operation affects your employees, your customer, your community, and the environment.[16]

There are also legal structures that B Corporations must follow. Your governing documents will need to be amended to make clear that your board of directors is responsible for balancing purpose and profit in their guidance of the business. Plus, you must regularly issue public reports that assess your business's social and environmental performance.

There are over four thousand certified B Corporations around the globe and across industries—including Ben and Jerry's, Eileen Fisher, Seventh Generation, Bombas, Thrive Market, and Patago-

---

16 "Measuring a Company's Entire Social and Environmental Impact." B Corporation. Accessed May 11, 2022. https://www.bcorporation.net/en-us/certification.

nia—all of whom choose this organizing structure to hold their business to a higher standard than just profit.

HOLACRACY

In the nineties, the agile software development movement emerged and brought forward a self-managing, collaborative way of developing software. This approach challenged the prevailing thinking of the day and ushered in a faster, more adaptive approach that considerably accelerated product and software development cycles. Holacracy was developed on the shoulders of the agile movement by Brian Robertson and others.

Holacracy offers a different way of organizing work in order to deliver value to the market. It offers an alternative to the default hierarchical approach. You can think of the purpose of any org structure and/or management system being to clearly answer these questions:

1. Who owns what?
2. Who gets to decide what?
3. What is the relationship between people?

Holacracy answers these by separating people from roles and job functions. Instead of being organized around a hierarchy of people, the company is organized around a hierarchy of purpose. The main idea behind the holacratic approach is that today's increasingly complex environment requires an equally dynamic organizational structure in order to address new challenges and opportunities that emerge. It effectively does away with the traditional role of an all-powerful manager who is usually siloed inside a function. While it is possible to import some of the best ideas and innovations in a piecemeal approach ("holacracy lite"), the holacratic charter is generally adopted as a wholesale replacement for the traditional organizational structure.

Key features of holacracy:

- It offers a new way for defining who is responsible for what and provides clarity on accountability.
- It outlines a clear definition of who has authority over what business assets.
- It has a system and process for defining and then evolving the governance structure.
- It has a set of processes and structures that address both the execution of the work at the operational level and a way of evolving the role definitions, which include decision rights and authority (veto power).

Hundreds of companies have adopted a holacratic approach to business that orients toward self-managing teams at every level as well as a self-managing organization. For more information on the holacratic approach, go to https://www.holacracy.org.

WHAT DOES YOUR ORGANIZATIONAL STRUCTURE INCENTIVIZE?

New modalities, like B Corporations and Holacracy, are intriguing because there is perhaps no greater influencer of culture than how a company chooses to formalize power, ownership, and decision-making rights.

The structure of a company predetermines much of what is incentivized and—in the case of most corporations—much of what is incentivized is often out of alignment with the espoused values. For example, the default purpose of most corporations is to maximize shareholder value. The majority of shares are held by founders and early investors. So while most companies want to cultivate a culture where there is a shared "sense of ownership" (a cultural value), at the most fundamental level, actual ownership is concentrated amongst a small number of people. Stock grants and employee ownership programs may nibble at the edges, but they usually account for only a tiny percentage of actual equity. How do you cultivate a sense of shared ownership in a company that is majority owned by less than five people? These are the impacts of your organizational structure and important considerations as you embed your culture into your company.

Admittedly, the decision of what kind of corporate and org structure you will have is not one you make often, but it is worth considering. By contrast, the final culture-embedding strategy we cover in this chapter is something that every leader has regular control over and is something you can influence daily.

Individual and Leadership Behaviors

As leaders, our actions speak louder than words. If you aren't living your values in the day-to-day work, then you're inviting skepticism not only of yourself as a leader but also of your values and the culture as a whole. You simply cannot scale your culture if your values say one thing and your actions say another.

Your and your leaders' behaviors are the most important place to embed your values.

Hopefully, during the Prototype step, you already experienced the value of creating explicit agreements on behaviors within your leadership team. The most committed leadership teams continue that effort during the embedding process, taking the opportunity to agree on a set of specific ways of being that they'll individually and collectively exhibit as they guide the organization.

Three things will help you and your team:

1. Define the specific, observable behaviors that you want all leaders to adopt and practice.
2. Include these behaviors as part of your manager competencies and performance management rubric.
3. Offer coaching and training to help leaders get better at these skills.

One executive team that we worked with identified "Show Up with Curiosity" as their value that, while appropriate, felt the most difficult for them to live out. As a group, they explored specific behaviors that they could practice together and an agreed-upon way to give each other feedback to improve. The protocol focused on people *asking* for feedback regularly. They found that when people asked, it was a *lot* easier to provide simple feedback. In one-on-one meetings, managers would ask people to self-report on the number of times in the last two weeks that they asked for feedback and the number of times they had offered feedback. It was a bold commitment that pushed them to embed their values into an increasing number of conversations.

Another company, a five-hundred-plus-person Series D company, trains their entire team using a workshop called "How to Hybrid," which addresses how they are committed to working in a post-pandemic, partially remote workplace. The workshop teaches employees how to work in a hybrid work environment and includes at least two culture-reinforcing behaviors. This experience will touch every employee in the company and provide everyone with a common approach and language.

What you commit to for individual behaviors will of course be unique to your company, your culture, and your values, but don't skip making explicit expectations here as you embed your culture.

HOW TO START EMBEDDING

Now it's your turn. Convene a meeting to discuss where you are already embedding culture and determine what your greatest opportunities are to do more. Use the list above as a starting point. What are some of the "low-hanging fruit"—the opportunities—that will be easy to implement and have the biggest impact?

Create an action plan to embed your values in one or two of the areas mentioned above within the next three months. For each

EXAMPLE CULTURE WORKFLOW

	FEB	MAR	APR	MAY	JUN
Essence & Shadows	Discovery focus groups	Distill & refine themes			
Executive Team		CEO leads drafting of values; exec team finalizes	Executive team prototyping	Executive team debrief prototyping experiment	
Internal Comms	Announce culture process email from CEO	People team to launch weekly newsletter for regular home for culture and company updates	CEO to share update and explain rationale behind prototyping		
All-Hands	1. Culture process reminder 2. Attendees participate in focus groups			1. Unveil values 2. Small group discussion to connect with values and brainstorm ideas for bringing them to life	
Performance Management				Culture team + VP of people to lead review and updating of current process	
Recruiting			Culture team + head of talent to reorient the interview process to evaluate against each value		
Onboarding			Culture team + head of talent to embed values in post-accept, week one, and month one workflows		
Goal-Setting/ Strategic Planning					Q3 OKR setting —include at least one culture objective
Platforms & Tools				Culture team to evaluate opps for embedding culture	Begin rolling out changes to tools
Board Management	Share rationale and hopes for culture process at quarterly board meeting			1. Introduce and discuss culture code at quarterly board meeting 2. Are there any updates to our regular board meeting agenda to embed our culture?	
Pulse Survey					Send first pulse survey to evaluate current state vs. our named values
Manager 101 Training			Develop Manager & Culture-Building 101 workshop (Amplify)		Pilot Manager & Culture-Building 101 workshop

Here is an example of a roadmap we created
for one Series C Company that was about to hire
one hundred people in the next nine months

item, assign an owner and have them lead a design sprint to start the embedding process. If you aren't familiar with design sprints and how to use them, GV (formerly Google Ventures) offers an excellent how-to guide online at https://www.gv.com/sprint. To give owners time to run their design sprints, schedule a follow-up meeting for about a month from now to review progress and make adjustments.

Embedding culture is a never-ending process. Each stage of your company's growth will bring a new set of opportunities to integrate your Culture Code into the different parts of your business. In the early stages, most of the culture-building initiative needs to be generated by the founders and/or a small leadership team. But as your business grows and as you add more people, your team of "culture-builders" will eventually expand to include everyone in the company. We'll start this process in the next chapter, as we amplify your culture.

CHECKLIST FOR THE EMBED STEP

Create touchpoints with your Culture Code by embedding your values across three dimensions of your business.

The I dimension: Creating clear personal commitments to living your Culture Code
- ☐ Define specific, observable behaviors for all leaders to model and practice.
- ☐ Fold those behaviors into your manager competencies and performance feedback system.

The WE dimension: Strengthening interpersonal bonds through shared values
- ☐ Amplify existing rituals at the company and establish new rituals for times when people gather. Use these as moments where your values can be experienced as a group.
- ☐ Improve the quality of the conversations in your business.

The IT dimension: Turning your processes into daily cultural touchpoints
- ☐ Craft a hiring guide to systemize how you attract values-aligned people to your business and then screen candidates for those qualities during the interview process.
- ☐ Craft an onboarding experience that serves as a powerful introduction to your culture.
- ☐ Explore how your current org structure supports or doesn't support the culture that you're building.
- ☐ Consider other high-leverage processes, like how you manage performance, the tools that you use and how you use them, your public brand, and how you include culture in your strategic decision-making.

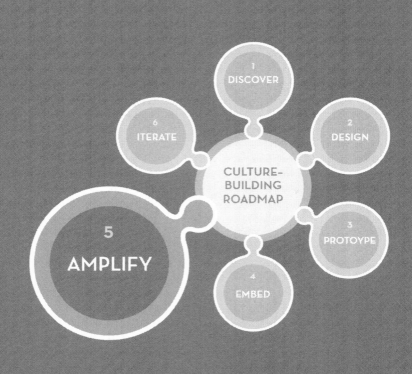

AMPLIFY

Culture-building isn't just a founder thing, or CEO thing, or HR thing; it's on everyone to make it happen.

BEWARE OF THE "CULTURE BLIND SPOT"

In a company with a culture blind spot, founders and leaders have heard that culture is important, they may believe that culture is important, and they might even say that culture is important, but they don't fully comprehend what culture *really is* and therefore fail to make it a top priority.

There are two main mindsets that leaders have that result in culture being pushed to the side or ignored altogether. The first is that of the results-oriented leader. Leaders who believe that results are all that matters—what Stephen Covey refers to as "the tyranny of the urgent"—remain focused on the whirlwind of emergencies, deadlines, and other short-term goals, at the expense of focusing on long-term results, like culture.

The second mindset to watch out for is one that reduces culture to a thing or an object that HR should do, rather than a complex social system that requires participation from everyone. When culture is unconsciously reduced to a quarterly goal or dismissed in the face of business demands, it is a clear sign that culture is not being taken seriously enough. This is a form of cultural reductionism on the part of the leaders.

As a result of this thinking, most companies rely on one well-meaning, but often extremely busy, person to keep the flame lit for culture-building efforts. This approach is not only slow, but also risks culture efforts coming to a halt whenever that person gets busy on other deliverables (or worse, leaves the company).

Instead you're going to dial up the impact of your culture by keeping culture conversations front and center in your work while also enlisting more and more of the team in culture-building.

ADOPT A CULTURE IN ACTION MINDSET

The idea of culture in action is a concept we first heard from Greg

Ranstrom[17]—founder of We, Inc. and WiWoW—and is an incredibly helpful mindset for amplifying culture.

A "culture in action moment" is simply any moment when your stated principles and values are being visibly demonstrated. These moments are happening all the time, but tend to be overlooked. With the nature of how human perception works, we tend not to notice things that we aren't looking for. So, to amplify your culture, you create reasons to pay attention to these moments—to notice, reflect and, talk about what's working and what's not (more on this in the next chapter)—and most importantly, to celebrate your culture as it unfolds.

Greg describes this best:

> *Right now, your organization is experiencing a variety of tensions. They're the inevitable gaps between where you are and where you want to be. They reflect the pull that's constantly at play in any healthy, growing, changing organization—between past and future, between competing visions for the future, between different approaches for getting from here to there.*
>
> *Tensions aren't problems. They are the source of all growth.*
>
> *There's no "right" answer to tensions. But how you handle them matters. And because organizations are made up of human beings, the solutions aren't just technical. There is a social component to almost every opportunity and obstacle you face.*
>
> *With every interaction, your culture evolves. As new people join, as others leave, your culture adapts. Every time you come together to confront a challenge, you*

---

17   "Culture in Action." Accessed May 11, 2022. https://www.cultureinaction.online/.

update the unwritten rules that define how your organiza-
tion works.

Adopting a "culture in action" mindset means accepting that *all* moments are potential culture moments to notice, learn from, and celebrate.

"Culture in action" moments include:

- How you make and communicate decisions
- How you respond to negative customer feedback
- How you decide and communicate changes in process, approach, or strategy
- How people navigate differences of opinion and conflict
- How you part with people leaving your team
- How you conduct leadership team meetings or all-hands meetings (whenever three or more are gathered)

Adopting a "culture in action" mindset is like putting on a pair of magical glasses that allows you to see the cultural dimension of everything that happens in your business. Seeing your team and company through this lens is the first step.

INCREASE THE NUMBER OF CULTURE-BUILDERS

The second step is to increase the number of people who are paying attention to culture—not as a separate activity, but as a part of the work.

Set the expectation that everyone is a culture-builder. Train your people on how to notice and initiate "culture in action" moments every day.

A culture-builder is someone who chooses to intentionally shape and influence the culture of their team or company. Regardless of their role, they acknowledge the influence they already have on others and choose to harness that influence in service of creating a better group experience.

Increasingly, we are seeing that within the companies that are most successful at scaling culture, leaders at all levels embrace the role of culture-builder. Yes, there is still a senior leader willing to be accountable for maintaining focus over time. But they have a team of culture-builders behind them.

While working on a culture-building effort with a growing biotech company recently, there came a time when the leaders expressed a sincere desire to build a truly impactful culture but also a concern that more buy-in would be needed to realize their vision. They invited a pool of managers into a conversation focused solely on their culture. It became clear quite quickly that they had a lot of people who already had a natural inclination for culture-building and most, if not all, of the necessary skills to do it. Their team just needed a little inspiration and someone to give them permission to step up and lead in this way.

Creating a company culture that is a source of pride is an ongoing, never-ending effort. The more culture-builders you have, the more successful your culture-building effort will be over the long term. More culture-builders equals better results. Amplifying is about engaging exactly these people inside your organization.

CREATE A COMPANY CULTURE LAUNCH

If you have already completed the Prototype step and at least started the Embed step, then you will likely have sufficient confidence in your leadership team's ability to demonstrate the culture in action, and you will have already taken steps to make it real and visible. Now it's time to go public with it.

A "culture launch" is part product launch, part ritual celebration, and part culture-builder basic training. Done right, a culture launch can become a defining moment in the company's history and lore, a galvanizing experience that people will refer back to fondly for years to come.

In your culture launch, your goal is to create a reference touch-point for each of the values. You also want to create an experience that every employee will remember for a long time and ideally something that can be embedded into your onboarding for future employees too.

You can do this by creating a company-wide gathering or a repeatable workshop that demonstrates the culture you are endeavoring to live.

There is no one right way to do this. It can be as easy extending one of your next all-hands, like Cricket Health did, *or* you can create a stand-alone all-day gathering and celebration, as companies like Tile and Montoux did after they created their first Culture Code.

The goal of this event/gathering/workshop is to accomplish three things:

1. Introduce a common way of thinking about culture—one that is both practical and actionable. Our in-house version of this talk is called "Culture 101," and it covers "What is culture?", "What are the levers that shape culture?", and "What can each person do to help shape the culture of the company?"

2. Give people a chance to assess their own behavior through the lens of the Culture Code. One way to do this is to ask each individual to do some self-reflection in a journal on questions like:
   > For you, which of our values feel easiest to live by? Which ones feel most challenging?
   > Within your team, where are you already being consistent with the Culture Code? Where are you not being consistent with the culture values?

After journaling, create time for sharing within the group. Your leadership team, in particular, should have stories worth sharing from practicing living your culture during the Prototype step. For an example of a personal culture inventory you can use, go to the Resources section at www.scalewithoutlosingyoursoul.com.

3. For each value, give people a reference experience to show them what it looks like / sounds like / feels like to live the value versus not living the value. Some ways you can do this include:

   › Offering a mini-training module on a specific skill. For example, at a recent company culture launch, to reinforce the value of "Always Learning," everyone was taught a specific practice on asking for and being open to feedback. Everybody left that session with a common language and approach for a very important culture-reinforcing behavior.

   › Have the group brainstorm specific dos and don'ts for each culture principle. For instance, at Tile's culture launch, everyone broke into cross-functional groups and brainstormed different ways to implement and practice each of the values (one group per value) and then reported back to the large group.

   › You may also have key leaders give examples through storytelling (prepared in advance) of what it means to live each of the values.

Doing at least one of these can enhance the depth and practicality of your culture launch.

In addition, your company's origin story, vision, mission, and customer stories can all help contribute to a more holistic experience of your company's essence/culture.

Eventually, a version of this training/culture event can become part of every new hire's onboarding experience so that every team member is empowered and equipped to be a culture-builder in their corner of the world.

For a more comprehensive view of what a culture launch can look like, we've include a sample in the Resources section at www. scalewithoutlosingyoursoul.com.

KEEP CULTURE FRONT AND CENTER

It's not enough to talk about values and show pretty slides. You need to find a way to bring these values to life by creating regular, repeatable rituals where culture is the focus.

How to Create Regular, Repeatable Rituals Where Culture Is the Focus

Build in time at regular leadership team and company meetings and gatherings to focus on culture: ten minutes at a monthly all-hands meeting, or five minutes at a weekly leadership meeting, or even a couple hours at an annual company retreat. One client of ours has a "culture corner" in their widely read monthly internal newsletter, where people share examples of "culture in action" moments from the past month.

In the early days at Tumblr, the company had two guiding values: "Fuck Yeah" (which was about excellence) and "Humblr" (which was about honoring unsung heroes). When I arrived at their offices for the first time, the welcome mat to their third-floor New York City office said "Fuck Yeah" and they gave a monthly award to two employees (nominated and voted on by their peers) who most embodied each of the values that month.

Another small startup we worked with this last year will play a ten-minute "game" every once in a while that helps the group appreciate the good parts of their team culture. The game consists of a simple sentence stem that people take turns filling in: "One thing I appreciate about us (i.e., this team, this company, our culture) is..."

It goes something like this:

> *"Something I appreciate about us is that we have each other's backs."*

> *"Something I appreciate about us is how we don't blame anyone else when we have issues."*

> *"Something I appreciate about us is how into our product we are."*

As you can imagine, after ten minutes of this, the vibe and connectedness of the group is powerfully strong.

Consider Setting Up Slack Reacji Channeler to Highlight Culture Moments

As we previously mentioned, if your team uses Slack to communicate, there's an incredibly useful app called Reacji Channeler that makes it simple to highlight and make visible culture-building efforts. When a reacji (emoji reaction) occurs on a message, the message is automatically routed into another channel where the right people can see and act upon it.

Our suggestions:

1. Create custom emojis for each value.
2. Create value channels (e.g., #value-NAME).
3. Install and set up Reacji Channeler so that anytime one of your custom culture emojis is used, that message gets routed to the appropriate value channel.

AN EXAMPLE OF A TEAM'S CUSTOM EMOJIS

A few ideas for using Reacji Channeler:

- When a customer quote is posted in #team-marketing, someone could react with the 🖤 emoji to route the quote to a corresponding value channel related to serving your customers.
- When a team accomplishes something significant that's shared in their team channel, reacting with the ⭐ emoji could route to a #wins channel.
- Use 📢 to route any notifications that everyone should be aware of to an #announcements channel.

```
#  value-candor
#  value-committed-to-learning
#  value-complexity-to-simplicity
#  value-curiousity
#  value-forward-in-action
#  value-play
#  value-respect
#  value-win-win
```

Examples of value channels

A more comprehensive guide on how to use Slack to enhance culture is also available in the Resources section at www.scalewith-outlosingyoursoul.com.

FORM YOUR CULTURE CORE TEAM

One of the best approaches we have seen to amplifying culture efforts and keeping them front and center is to form a cross-functional Culture Core Team.

Different companies call it different things: Culture Champions, Wisdom Team, Culture in Action Team. It doesn't matter what you call it. What matters is that you prioritize culture enough to make it a top-five priority and back that up by empowering key employees and leaders to invest their time in your Culture Core Team.

In 2014, Katie Hunt-Morr led Etsy's version of a Culture Core Team. Internally, the team was known as the Values and Impact Team. She described its purpose as follows:

> *The biggest advice I have is that culture needs to be a cross-company effort. The key to getting employees to buy into it was to look at the projects that were already going on in the company and explore how we can embed our values into what we do within those projects.*
>
> *As the company grew really quickly, it's difficult to have the osmotic transfer that naturally happened. That's why we formed the "Values and Impact Team" whose purpose is to give all employees the means and desire to embody the company values in all of their daily work.*

At Asana—a workplace-productivity management company—representatives from all areas of the company meet regularly to evaluate how they are doing at living their values and create new ways to embed values into every process in the company.

Ev Williams, co-founder and current CEO at Medium, once said, "If you want something to happen, you must have someone whose job it is to pay attention to that." To heed this advice, we recommend you do these two things:

1. Establish a single culture owner who is ultimately responsible for leading ongoing culture efforts.
2. Form the culture team from a cross section of people from different teams and functions, and have them meet on a regular basis.

Establishing a culture owner and Culture Core Team will keep culture front and center and part of the conversation as you scale.

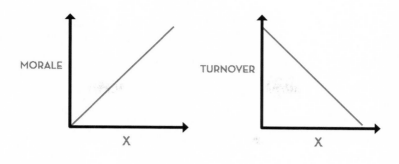

X = Culture-builders empowered

CALLING ALL CULTURE-BUILDERS

How many active culture-builders do you have in your company right now? How many people can you honestly say are actively paying attention to how culture is scaling as your company grows? What would it take to double or triple that number?

The more culture-builders you have, the more people you have bringing their best selves to difficult moments and inviting others to join them. And the more people you have practicing the culture, the stronger your culture gets. To succeed at building and sustaining a thriving culture, everyone must be involved. The Amplify step is all about enrolling others in culture-building.

CHECKLIST FOR THE AMPLIFY STEP

This step is about enlisting your entire organization in continually building your desired culture.

During the Amplify step:

- ☐ Adopt a "culture in action" mindset, turning every moment into an opportunity to reinforce your culture.
- ☐ Celebrate a culture launch to explain and train your team on your newly articulated Culture Code and how it will be lived within the organization.
- ☐ Enroll leaders, at every level at the company, to be culture-builders.
- ☐ Form your culture cross-functional team to drive new culture initiatives and experiments forward.

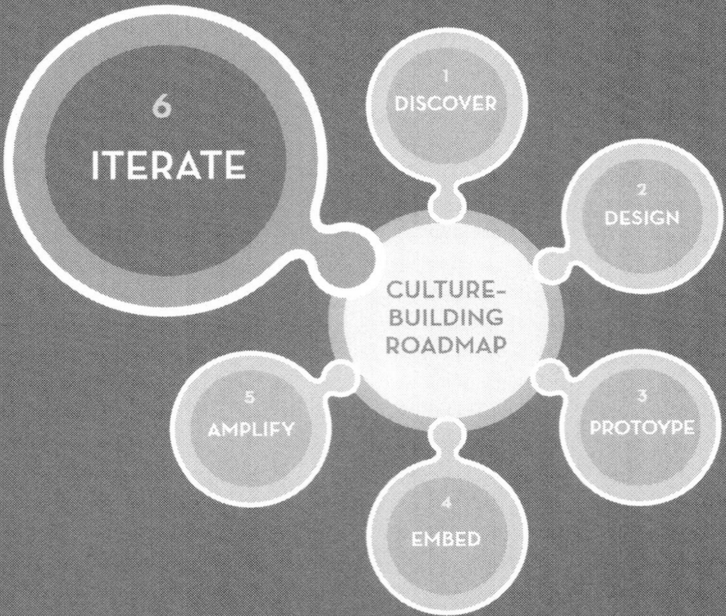

6 ITERATE

1 DISCOVER

2 DESIGN

3 PROTOYPE

4 EMBED

5 AMPLIFY

CULTURE-BUILDING ROADMAP

ITERATE

"Your company's culture is one
of its product offerings."

—BIZ STONE, CO-FOUNDER OF TWITTER

After undertaking a culture effort, most teams let the conversation about culture fade into the background. Your culture-building efforts to this point become merely a completed project. Your work on culture will have some short-term positive effects, but the gains will deteriorate over time.

Scaling a company demands attention. If culture-building isn't core to your strategy, then it will always lose out to the company's other demands.

You were diligent in discovering your essence and designing a Culture Code that articulates that essence in a clarifying, energizing way. Then you stress tested your Culture Code by prototyping with your team to ensure that you could "walk the talk." With confidence in your Culture Code, you embedded your values throughout the day-to-day work and enlisted your broader team to amplify your desired culture. It's been quite a project up to this point.

Now you move from treating culture like a project to treating culture as a product.

CULTURE AS PRODUCT

A *Fast Company* article shared Asana founders Dustin Moskovitz and Justin Rosenstein's approach to treating culture as a product:

> *Instead of looking at culture as something that "just happens," [they] realized that culture was actually something that needed to be carefully designed, tested, debugged, and iterated on, like any other product they released...*
>
> *"We actively survey people anonymously, and during one-on-ones, we ask what's working well and what isn't working well. Based on that information, we go back to the company*

and say, here's what we heard, and here's what we're going to do about it."[18]

It's not a coincidence that Asana routinely wins awards for being one of the best places in the world to work, including being named a Glassdoor Best Places to Work in back-to-back years.[19] A full 98 percent of employees would recommend working at Asana to a friend, and 100 percent approve of the CEO.

The very best product organizations focus relentlessly on finding ways to better serve their customers. They take time to understand what success looks like. Then they measure their effectiveness and use those learnings to inform what they work on next. This cycle of iteration enables the creation of world-changing products.

Your company culture should be treated no differently. It is your second product.

And in the same way that products are continually improved, you'll continually improve your culture through these three phases: Build, Measure, and Learn.

The faster the flywheel turns, the more impact you'll get from your culture.

You can think of creating the first version of your Culture Code as completing your first Build phase. Next, you'll turn toward measuring your culture to create feedback loops for learning and then finally deciding on next actions and experiments to build.

---

18 Lorenz, Taylor. "How Asana Built The Best Company Culture In Tech." Fast Company, March 29, 2017. https://www.fastcompany.com/3069240/how-asana-built-the-best-company-culture-in-tech.

19 "Asana Named Top 5 Best Workplaces by Great Place to Work® and FORTUNE for the Fourth Year in a Row." Asana, January 28, 2020. https://asana.com/press/releases/pr/asana-named-top-5-best-workplaces-by-great-place-to-work-and-fortune-for-the-fourth-year-in-a-row/b4a17035-d91e-41ea-80e0-02d54decod9f.

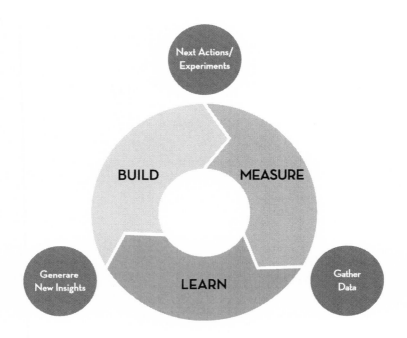

HOW TO MEASURE YOUR CULTURE

Start by setting up methods for measuring your culture so that actionable data is readily available to cut through the nuance of your culture. We want as clear a picture as possible of how your culture is (and isn't) working. A mix of both qualitative and quantitative information works best here.

Value-Specific Quantitative Metrics

Often there are values in your Culture Code that lend themselves to having metrics directly tied to your effectiveness in honoring those values.

Walk through your Culture Code and see which values lend themselves to being tracked with focused metrics.

Here are a few examples of how this might look:

- HubSpot's stated value "We Look to the Long Term and Solve for the Customer" might involve customer satisfaction and correlated customer retention scores.
- Lululemon's "Training Our Employees in Self-Responsibility and Goal Setting" might be tracked by noting trends in individual OKR scores over time.
- Google's "Fast Is Better than Slow" could be measured internally through work velocity and externally through performance benchmarks of their products.

You don't need to concoct metrics for every one of your values. But don't miss out on leveraging easily available data.

Keeping these sorts of metrics front and center not only gives you a pulse on how well you're honoring a value, but also creates natural culture-building conversations (e.g., "What might we try next to positively impact this?").

Capturing Broader Data through Surveys

Short surveys are another simple, proactive way to capture data on your culture. And it has never been easier to set up an efficient, regular feedback loop. Many digital work platforms (15Five, Lattice, and Culture Amp, to name a few) make it very easy to deploy surveys that take a few minutes to respond to. If you're more of a do-it-yourselfer, survey tools like Typeform, SurveyMonkey, or Google Forms will work just fine too.

There are two surveys we suggest running for your team: pulse surveys and deep dives.

PULSE SURVEYS

As the name might suggest, these surveys help you keep a pulse on how the people on your team are doing and feeling. Since you should aim to capture the good, the bad, and the ugly in these surveys, it's important to make them completely anonymous.

Run pulse surveys frequently (once every 1–3 months) to give you regular feedback and create a trendline to spot changes in sentiment and/or engagement, but not too frequently to cause survey fatigue. Sometimes a single event where a value wasn't honored can impact a wide swath of people. Other times trends play out more slowly. In either case, pulse surveys help you spot opportunities on the regular.

Not only do you get data from the responses submitted, but the percentage of people who respond to these surveys can also give you an idea of how engaged the team is. Team members who are not willing to make time to help improve the company are themselves a signal that something is off culturally.

To help you get started, we've included some of our favorite pulse survey questions in the Resources section at www.scalewithoutlosingyoursoul.com.

DEEP-DIVE SURVEYS

We also suggest running a deep-dive survey annually to gather feedback from your entire team. This is a full, 360-degree health check on your culture. Use quantitative questions to create benchmarks to compare against over time. Use qualitative questions to elicit more detailed perspectives from each person. You'll want to ask questions about the culture as a whole, plus zoom in on each of your values to understand how alive each individual value is in your organization.

In order to drive increased engagement, we have found that it is crucial for senior leaders to make a live announcement at an all-hands to provide the reasoning for "why this is important" and to ask the entire team to prioritize investing time in filling out the survey.

Examples of effective deep-dive survey questions are also included in the Resources section at www.scalewithoutlosingyoursoul.com.

ARE THE RIGHT PEOPLE STAYING?

"Bored people quit."
—Michael Lopp, VP of product engineering at Slack

When good people are leaving your organization, something is wrong. It may be boredom, or it could be something worse. Either way, retention numbers show you how your culture is perceived. Be warned, though, employee retention is a heavily lagging indicator. By the time people start heading for the door en masse, something went sideways culturally a while ago. Still, retention— especially of your top talent—should always be a key result and measurable of an effective culture.

Make a point to learn from every departure. When someone leaves the company, hold exit interviews with them. Appreciate their time on the team and inquire about their experience. Most departing employees—especially those in effective cultures—will pour back into the culture by sharing the things that could have been better in their experience. This information is incredibly valuable for you. Thank them for any and all insights.

If you don't get candor during an exit interview, that's also data indicating a cultural issue. Departing team members who aren't willing to share at least some of their authentic experience should set off alarm bells. They are feeling closed off from either you or the company. You either hired the wrong person or you have a culture that has left this person feeling disconnected. Both situations require attention.

If you hired the wrong person, then you'll want to find better ways to embed your culture in your hiring process.

This is a lack of "culture fit" on full display. Without resonance between your company's values and the values of each person who joins your team, you can expect ongoing employee underperformance and churn.

If they're feeling disconnected from you or the company, then there's also work to do. A conversation with their manager is a starting point. What signals did they have that this person might be feeling disconnected? What made it challenging for the employee to surface their concerns sooner? What cultural learnings can you take away from this?

HOW TO CREATE FEEDBACK LOOPS TO DRIVE LEARNING

As measurable culture data comes in, it's essential to set up feedback loops to guide the learning process. A big part of this effort is simply carving out regular, repeated time for learning.

Keeping Culture on the Agenda

The simplest way to set up regular feedback loops is to get recurring time on people's calendars. These are often the highest-leverage meetings on anyone's calendar, so don't let them be left to chance or fall into the trap of thinking that "no one needs another meeting." Keeping culture on the agenda means prioritizing time.

We suggest scheduling a monthly or bimonthly meeting for your Culture Core Team (your cross-functional team set up in the Amplify step). In advance of these meetings, share key metrics and the most recent pulse survey data to give everyone ample time to process the data. Consider including one or two prompts to help focus the conversation.

Example prompts:

- *What data stood out the most from our last survey?*
- *If we focus on one aspect of our culture at this meeting, what would you suggest?*
- *Where is our culture strong? Where is there room for improvement?*
- *What have you noticed about our culture and how we work together since our last meeting?*
- *What is one way we might make our values come alive more during this next cycle?*

Beyond your Culture Core Team meeting, the teams with the strongest cultures can integrate similar conversations into their daily and weekly meetings, even if just for a few minutes. Different companies have their own styles for holding learning conversations around culture, so find the right cadence for you and your team.

At Asana, for example, the entire company takes a full week off from business to roadmap company goals (which include reviewing and updating culture-related goals) *every* quarter:

> *When problems are brought to the table, Rosenstein says that management is quick to address the issues. Asana even has a name for these issues—"culture bugs"—and it seeks to squash them as quickly as bugs in the codebase of any other product.*[20]

---

20 Lorenz, Taylor. "How Asana Built The Best Company Culture In Tech." Fast Company, March 29, 2017. https://www.fastcompany.com/3069240/ how-asana-built-the-best-company-culture-in-tech.

Two actions to take right now:

1. Consider adjusting your leadership team (and other team) meeting agendas to create time for conversations like these. Even short bits of time can be foundational for letting cultural feedback flow.
2. Prioritize time now for ongoing culture work. Get the meetings on the calendar. They can always be rescheduled, but too often they never get scheduled in the first place.

Use Plus/Delta (+/Δ) Retrospectives to Surface Learnings

Facilitated retrospectives can be a useful tool for efficiently surfacing learning opportunities within your Culture Core Team or leadership team. We like to use a two-column framework called Plus/Delta for this to easily identify what's going well (+) and what you might change (Δ).

Create two columns on a whiteboard. Label one + and the other Δ. Set a timer for 3–5 minutes and have each person write down things that are going well (the +s). Then have each person briefly share their answers, and add them to the + column on the board. As each subsequent person shares, group similar ideas together.

Then set a timer for 3–5 minutes again, and have each person write down things that might change (the Δs). Again, have people share, and group ideas in the Δ column on the whiteboard.

Once all the topics are on the board, each person votes on the 2–3 that they believe could be the highest leverage to iterate on. These are things that are going well that we might dial up to be more impactful, or things that might be changed. Use dry-erase markers on a physical whiteboard or, if virtual, have each person type their initials next to an item.

This process will help you focus on the biggest opportunities for culture-building through next actions and experiments.

An Annual Entire-Company Culture Conversation

At least once a year, we suggest engaging the entire organization in a State of Our Culture conversation and brainstorm. The results you gather from your deep-dive survey are a natural input for this gathering. Plan an all-hands meeting during which you will share out the recent survey results and then hold a discussion.

During the all-hands, be sure to acknowledge and celebrate the good, while also talking openly about things that aren't going as well. There will be some topics that will be more appropriate for leadership to speak to and share plans on. These could be company strategy questions or concerns on leadership behaviors.

There should also be opportunities to bring everyone into a conversation on how to create more meaning and impact together. For example, if there's feedback from the deep-dive survey that your onboarding could be more effective, this might be a powerful focus area for everyone to contribute thinking on. To do this, use small breakout sessions to let people brainstorm and vote on ideas. Then have each team bring their 1–2 favorite suggestions back to the group. Not only do you get everyone bought in and engaging with your culture, but you will also have moments when something that is shared is so resonant that you can feel the vibe shift to be more proactive and positive.

DECIDE ON NEXT ACTIONS AND EXPERIMENTS

Whether in your Culture Core Team, at your annual State of Our Culture conversation, with your leadership team, or in your own actions, your focus is on taking learnings and developing next actions and experiments to run. This is culture-building. Imagine new possibilities ("What if we..."), craft experiments to test their impact, and identify someone to be accountable for measuring the results.

Through experimentation like this, a West Coast media agency sparked an entire *taco economy* within their organization simply by experimenting with a Slack application called HeyTaco.[21] Each team member could give a virtual taco anytime as kudos for people living out their values, and acquired tacos could be spent on a variety of things (catered lunches, swag, treats, etc.). The experiment was so successful that the team was always on the lookout for new, interesting ways to expand the impact of giving regular recognition to one another through the taco economy.

Another team, iterating on their value of "Always Being Open to New Ideas," might try holding a no-bad-ideas brainstorm session and inviting the entire organization to bring their best (and worst) ideas to the table.

Framing new approaches to culture-building as experiments has two big benefits. First, it creates a lightness around things that don't work. When something fails, toss it in the trash bin and try something else. Second, experiments help force ongoing conversation about what is or isn't working.

With any experiment or next action, identify an owner, and ensure they have the resources needed to move forward.

Ideally these initiatives can be folded into your existing business processes. There's benefit to culture work being prioritized right alongside other business needs. For example, if HubSpot's customer satisfaction scores (tied to their value "We Look to the Long Term and Solve for the Customer") begin to drop, customer-facing members of the Culture Core Team might engage their teams to reprioritize or reimagine initiatives aimed at impacting that metric in the coming months. If using existing workstreams isn't feasible, establish an owner within the Culture Core Team to drive the experiment or initiative forward.

---

21 "Build Stronger, Happier, Thriving Teams." HeyTaco. Accessed May 11, 2022.
    https://www.heytaco.chat/.

WHEN CULTURE-BUILDING GETS MESSY

You're going to screw up. People will misbehave. Someone will say the wrong thing. Gossip will happen. It's not supposed to be easy or clean. Embrace it all. Learn from it. And when necessary, clean it up.

Things got messy at a company that one of us founded a few years ago. We had a team of great people, but revenue wasn't growing as quickly as our projections had forecast. We needed to reduce burn to give ourselves time to sort out the path forward. We made the hard decision to lay off a large part of the team. A group of us stayed up deep into the night, planning each and every step of how we were going to share the news and do our best to support both the people leaving the team and those staying.

The next morning I woke up to two text messages.

First, a panicked text from my co-founder:

We need to talk ASAP. (Our sales leader) told the sales team half of them were getting let go. (Different person, not on the sales team) is talking to other people about being let go. What the f—.

The second, a response from our CRO:

F—, I literally told them four times to not share any changes.

I hurried to the office for damage control. When I arrived, I went for a walk with our sales leader to understand what exactly had been shared and why. Upon inquiring into his sharing the news with the team, he pointed to one of our values as his rationale: "We Are Open and Honest with One Another."

In his mind, keeping impactful information from his team wasn't being open and honest.

But his line of thinking missed a second stated value: "We Care for Others." No one was feeling cared for that morning. We did our best from that point forward to be both open and honest and to care for people. Hard, honest conversations were had about our failure as leaders to guide the company's growth and the subsequent need for a layoff. There was confusion, anger, tears. It was hard. It also was a significant culture-building moment. The team that remained rallied around a new level of openness and honesty layered with caring for one another.

That tension between your values should forever spark debate and exploration—and sometimes clean-up. It's not always fun. But this is the raw material from which great companies are built.

If you determine that you missed the mark in your Culture Code, you can loop back to redesign it. More often, though, it's only a part of your Culture Code that needs to be reevaluated. If you're wrestling with a question like, "Do we really believe and live *this value*?" then go back to prototyping on that value specifically. Ask the team, "How can we put this value to the test through this team's actions in the coming weeks?" Uncover the deeper essence of what you value through actions, not debate.

THE FASTEST ITERATIVE LOOP: BUILDING CULTURE EVERY DAY

The ultimate culture hack is to make conversations about your culture a natural part of the day-to-day work. Any conversation where you pause and reflect together on *how* a conversation or situation just occurred makes room for insights about your culture's health and effectiveness. These "meta-conversations" can happen at the end of meetings, projects, quarters, or indeed anytime.

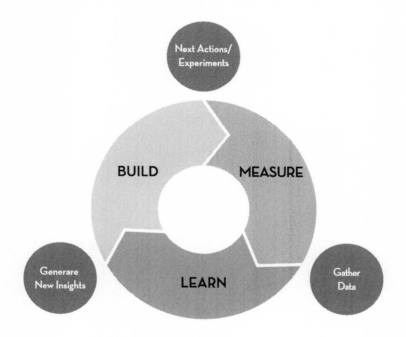

This is the fastest iterative loop available to you. It turns every day and every interaction into a culture-building opportunity. Noticing where you (individually or collectively) aren't living your values is new data available every day. Naming and talking about these moments allows you to learn from them and then perhaps make a new culture-building choice. It's the entire Build-Measure-Learn loop available in each and every interaction.

CHECKLIST FOR THE ITERATE STEP

Here you're choosing to treat your culture as not just a one-time project but the second product that you're building. You'll kick off an iterative Build-Measure-Learn loop to do this.

During the Iterate step:
- ☐ Set up measurables to determine the health and effectiveness of your culture. These might include metrics tied directly to values, team surveys, and employee retention data.
- ☐ Schedule regular retrospective meetings to process and learn from the data that you collect.
- ☐ Engage the entire company at least annually with a deep-dive survey and corresponding State of Our Culture all-hands meeting.
- ☐ Leverage your Culture Core Team to turn learnings into next actions and experiments to build.

CULTURE-BUILDING ROADMAP
A Proven Approach for Building a Company You Are Proud Of

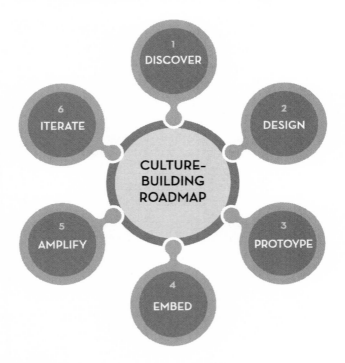

1 DISCOVER
Discover the living, breathing cultural essence that your team and company already has.

2 DESIGN
Design a Culture Code that is authentic, energizing, succinct, behaviorally explicit, and brand-reinforcing.

3 PROTOTYPE
Prototype living your culture within your leadership before rushing your Culture Code out the door.

4 EMBED
Embed your Culture Code throughout the organization: people processes, meeting rituals, decision-making, and the look & feel of your brand.

5 AMPLIFY
Amplify your desired culture by increasing the number of people acting as culture-builders in your company.

6 ITERATE
Iterate by deciding on the metrics you will use to track progress and continually improve. Culture-building, like product building, never ends.

COMMIT TO THE JOURNEY

You now have the entire *Culture-Building Roadmap*—the exact steps for scaling your business without losing your soul along the way.

1. First you **discover** your company's essence by engaging in an appreciative inquiry process. This is the raw material from which you define your culture.

2. You **design** a Culture Code that clarifies what matters most in a way that feels energizing, clarifying, and true to your essence.

3. With a first version of your Culture Code in hand, you **prototype** and test it within your leadership team first. You stress test your Culture Code by activating its guidance as a daily practice of behaviors and feedback.

4. Once you've proven your Culture Code, you **embed** your culture through individual behaviors, through rituals that create connection, and across all of the processes and systems within your organization.

5. As you scale and add more people, you can now **amplify** by increasing the number of culture-builders in your company from just a couple of founders to a much larger group.

6. Culture-building, like product-building, never ends. It's essential to **iterate**. You will be constantly testing, gathering feedback, learning new things, and updating your Culture Code and how it's expressed through new culture-building experiments.

This is the exact same process that we've used with startups like yours. In fact, when we were writing this book, one of the things we were asked multiple times was, "Are you sure you want to give away the secret sauce?" "This is what companies pay you to do. Why would you give it away?" and "Isn't this a bad business decision?"

But the truth is, it's not the *knowledge* of what to do that makes the difference. We know this because we have shared this with hundreds of leaders, and only a handful do much with the information. It turns out that the secret sauce is a combination of purpose, passion, and commitment. You have to want to build a special company. You have to be willing to carve out the time to put the work in. You have to be willing to give hard feedback when others are not living your values. And you have to be willing to look yourself in the mirror and be honest when you're falling short of that too. Only you can do this.

Right now you're at a crossroads.

One path forward is business as usual. Keep doing what you're doing. Grow the team, and grow revenue. And your company may end up succeeding. But along with this success will come the inevitable bureaucracy and power dynamics that typify most larger, soulless companies. The business will be the only thing that matters, and people will only stay because they think they have to or because they need a paycheck.

The other path takes commitment. It makes no promises, and yet it is filled with possibilities. You'll have a chance to build a company that you're truly proud of. A company that attracts the best and the brightest. A company that you yourself would want to work for. A company that matters—to your customers, to your investors, to your team members, and to our world.

What kind of company will you build?

Thank you for daring to be different. Know that you don't have to do this alone. We've created a resources section at www.scale-withoutlosingyoursoul.com that we'll continue to update. Plus, if there's any way we might be able to help you in your journey, you can always email us at simon@evolution.team and todd@evolution.team.

ADDITIONAL RESOURCES

To support your culture-building efforts, we've included a series of resources that we've found valuable and have used with our clients over the years, including:

- Interviews and articles by founders, venture capitalists, and culture thought leaders including Brian Chesky (Airbnb), Ray Dalio, Michael Lopp (Slack), and many others
- Sample pulse and deep dive surveys that you can use to measure your culture.
- Examples of some of our favorite company Culture Codes
- Our favorite books on culture, organizational design, and business scaling.
- Expanded guides on topics including:
  - › How to customize Slack to enhance culture
  - › How to use Zoom to enhance culture for virtual teams
  - › Scaling depth: Inspiration and instruction on how to create more connection and depth in a hybrid work environment
  - › How to pull off a great culture-launch event
- An FAQ with answers to questions like:

> We just raised a seed round, have eight people, and it's all hands on deck to survive. How can we focus on culture?
> We just closed a B-round after five successful quarters and feel like we have some wind at our back. We will hire one hundred new people this year. How much should we invest in our culture efforts?
> What if my team doesn't buy in?
> Where do I go for help?

Visit www.scalewithoutlosingyoursoul.com to learn more.

ACKNOWLEDGMENTS

From Simon:

Nine years ago, when I first embarked on the journey of writing this book, I had no idea that it would become what it is today. The journey that led to *this* book was less a straight road than a winding path.

The first three years were all about researching, interviewing, and capturing the stories that formed the basis for this book. Big thanks to the founders and culture-building trailblazers who participated in interviews and conversations, including Peter Block, Chip Conley, Pico Iyer, Pat Christen, Bob Hottman, Douglas Vilcheck (aka Yoda), Eric Friedman, Robert LoCasio, and Tony Hsieh (RIP).

To all the hosts and attendees of the many culture-builder dinners and gatherings where we explored this emerging field and exchanged ideas on the why and how of culture-building, including Jamie Woolf, Bria Martin, Jessica Amortegui, Josh Levine, and many others: I learned from each of you. And a special shoutout to Chris Marcell Murchison for being my co-collaborator in creating the culture-builder dinners, which for me is where it all began.

To the community of partners and coaches at Evolution: I have worked with more than six different consulting and coaching firms over the last 27 years, and this is the one where I can authentically say that we are walking our talk of "scaling without losing our soul."

To Todd, my coauthor, who showed up at just the right time and whose experience, collaboration style, and friendship have made these last four years fruitful and fun.

To my original "team"—my family:

Dad, for discovering the transformational scene in Southern California in the eighties and for letting it open your heart and transform your life (and therefore mine). You are a living example that deep transformation and change is possible.

My beloved wife, Tamra, for the big loving space you hold for me and others, and for knowing when to block my retreat. This book wouldn't exist without you.

To my daughters, Isabelle and Sophie, for all the ways you provided moral and practical support, including proofreading and feedback.

To my ad hoc writing support team, who encouraged and helped me along the way, including Steve Levin, Jonathan Robinson, Raven Wells, and Josh Levin.

Last but not least, to "ACT Team #1," my weekly accountability group: this book would not exist had it not been for the accountability structure of this group and the hundreds of weekly promises I made to write. Who said you can't write a book in thirty minutes a week?

From Todd:

This book is a result of decades of effort in trying to do work that matters both to myself and to others. Along the way, I've been supported and inspired by so many wonderful humans, a few of whom I want to acknowledge here.

First, to Matt Munson: without your dedication there would never have been a business nor a company culture to learn from. But most of all, for being the truest of friends.

To Steve Bull, Kevin Fremon, Michael Robinette, John Kempe, Jess McKenzie Mays, Micah Cohen, and the entire Twenty20 crew for being the place and team that showed me the true power—good, bad, and sometimes a bit ugly—of company culture.

To Shawn Grunberger at Bandcamp, Sean Goldfaden at CoEfficient Labs, Ammanuel Selameab at Accrue, Jen Henderson at Tilt, Taylor Margot at Keys, and Greg Sewitz and Gabi Lewis at Magic Spoon for gifting me with a unique vantage point into your own cultures as you've grown your companies.

To my family: Katie for being my rock, supporting me no matter what life brings. Harper and Clay for reminding me every day to explore and see the joy in life. Mom, Dad, Maureen, and Brett for always being a source of strength and stability.

To my partners and team at Evolution for being a community of practice and support that's helped me develop as both a person and a practitioner.

And finally, to my co-author, Simon D'Arcy. I can still recall standing in my backyard on the phone with you when you asked me if I wanted to write this book alongside you. I felt joy in that moment. I feel even more now and am deeply appreciative of you trusting me and this journey that we've undertaken together.

ABOUT THE AUTHORS

Between the two of us, we've experienced the impact of culture done well and culture done not so well across a wide variety of organizations.

TODD'S STORY

I've founded businesses my entire life.

The first was painting houses in my parents' neighborhood during high school. I made my own hours. I spent my summers in the sun, listening to music. I made more money in three months than my friends did working year-round at Subway. I was an entrepreneur, and I was hooked.

My most recent business was Twenty20, a venture-backed startup with investors including First Round Capital, Founders Fund, and Canaan Partners.

At Twenty20, I wanted so much to build a company that cared for and brought the best out of people. I wanted to build a team that supported each other in amazing ways. And, of course, I also wanted the company to be a successful business. But not at the expense of creating something that I wasn't proud of. The worst thing that could happen was building a financially successful company at the expense of people or myself. I wasn't willing to sacrifice that dream just for cash in my pocket.

And while the ideal was noble, the reality of building a venture-backed business was quite different. The product needed attention. Our go-to-market strategy wasn't defined. We needed to recruit new talent. There were new fires to put out weekly, if not daily.

I knew culture mattered but had no idea what to do about it.

I remember wishing for a guide that would just tell me what to do. This book is what I wish I could have handed to myself back then.

SIMON'S STORY

Over 25 years ago, when I joined a cadre of consultants at Malandro Communications, was when I first understood the power of company culture. Long before company culture was popular or main-stream, Dr. Loretta Malandro and her team were helping Fortune 1000 companies shift their culture from a command and control environment to a high-performance culture based on partnership, trust, and 100 percent accountability. This was the nineties and long before social media and companies like Glassdoor shifted the power balance between employers and employees—when most people tended to land a job and stay a long time. Here I learned how much influence and leverage a visionary CEO and senior team could have in shifting the culture of their enterprise.

I've seen both the best and the worst of what's possible in company cultures.

I have been part of company-wide culture transformation efforts at Fortune 500 companies, and I've helped early-stage startups discover and start to cultivate a cultural identity from their earliest days.

In 2013, I founded culture-builder.com—a resource site for culture-builders—and created the culture-builder dinner series as a way to create a community of practice for an increasing number of leaders who identified as culture-builders. We gathered, ate well, and shared lessons and challenges from doing culture work within organizations.

In 2015, I joined Evolution to support founders and startup leaders in designing and embedding more conscious and high-performing cultures that enabled greater purpose and better results. Since then, we have worked with over two hundred startups and fast-growing companies including companies like Slack, Dropbox, Bandcamp, Twitter, Snap, Iterable, and Glassdoor.

Each time I work with a new team of leaders, my basic thesis is affirmed: none of us live or work in a vacuum—yet people and teams act like they do. And as a result, the work world is fraught with an absence of accountability, avoidance of key issues, and polarized conversations. Meanwhile, we have complex problems to solve together. Business as usual—profit at all costs—isn't working. It's causing social and environmental damage faster than we can repair it.

I believe that the problems we face—as a team, company, or country—will require new ways of working together and founders and leaders willing to keep culture at the forefront of their approach and strategic initiatives. I feel called to support leaders who are committed to building a different type of company.

Made in the USA
Coppell, TX
26 January 2023

11735756R00092